Interpreting Dreams Dictionary

Edward Traut
Prophetic Life Ministry

© Copyright 2011 - Prophetic Life
Ministry
Third Edition
Printed in Canada

All rights reserved. This book is protected under the copyright laws of the United States of America. This book may not be copied or reprinted for commercial gain or profit.

All printed scripture references are from the New International Version of the Holy Bible, unless otherwise noted.

For information concerning conducting a workshop at your church, please contact our ministry office at 888-354-7770. Please feel free to contact us via email at propheticlife@me.com or visit our website at http://www.propheticlife.com for further information and additional available products.

Forward

The exploration of dreams is an adventure and a journey for each one of us individually as we discover the methods that God has assigned to us, the patterns of our dreaming and the way that God speaks to us individually.

This dictionary is designed to help you as a guideline, not to have perfect, clear answers that you rely on solely. This will help you as you begin to look up the different objects, colors and items that will help to direct you in the right path and possibly help in your dreaming. However, please be assured that not everything that you dream will be listed here. In addition, it is clear, that one item could mean more than one thing.

For example, a dog as we know in our culture, means a friend that is true to us. However, the scripture talks about a dog being on the outside or a dog returning to its vomit. So, as you can see this could mean several different things depending upon it's setting and situations or to different individuals.

It is important to understand that God uses the language of the Spirit to speak to individual people in the language that they are most accustomed to. For example, we find that when God spoke to Peter to go to Cornelius who was a gentile or "unclean", He gave Peter a vision of food. This met him right where he was in his state of physical hunger waiting for lunch or dinner to be prepared. The Lord could have used so many ways to communicate that the gentiles were not unclean or that he was to go to these people. But, this was the language that was closest to Peter's momentary life experience.

Therefore, I encourage you to use this dictionary but please be assured that not everything that is listed here may apply directly to you or be exactly always the same as your dream. So, use this book to help guide you but continue always an exploration through prayer and seeking the Lord. God will give you the understanding of your dreams and what each item means to you.

Table of Contents

Dream Symbols A	1
Dream Symbols B	12
Dream Symbols C	26
Dream Symbols D	34
Dream Symbols E	40
Dream Symbols F	44
Dream Symbols G	48
Dream Symbols H	51
Dream Symbols I	55
Dream Symbols J	57
Dream Symbols K	60
Dream Symbols L	62
Dream Symbols M	66
Dream Symbols N	73
Dream Symbols O	76
Dream Symbols P	79
Dream Symbols Q	84
Dream Symbols R	86
Dream Symbols S	95
Dream Symbols T	109
Dream Symbols U	121
Dream Symbols V	123
Dream Symbols W	127
Dream Symbols Y	135
Dream Symbols Z	136
Dream Colors	137
Dream Numbers	142

Interpreting Dreams Dictionary

Dream Interpretation Symbols

-A-

Acid - *Bitterness / Destruction / Dissolve*
   Positive - Dissolving of unhealthy things
   Negative - Poison, mockery, ridicule, gossip
   and foul speech, destruction, offense, hatred,
   sarcasm, revenge
   Mark 16:18, Acts 8:23, Heb. 12:15, Rom. 3:14

   Job 6:4 "The arrows of the Almighty are in me, my spirit drinks in their poison; God's terrors are marshaled against me"

Adultery - *Loss / Lack of Exclusivity*
   Betrayal, lack of covenant, Idolatry,
   double-minded, sin, may relate to
   spiritual adultery or physical adultery but more
   often relates to a state of mind or thought
   rather than a sexual sin.
   Jas. 4:4, Ex. 20:3; 20:14, Ez. 23:45

   Matt. 12:39 "He answered, "A wicked and adulterous generation asks for a miraculous sign! But none will be given it except the sign of the prophet Jonah."

Airplane - *Church / Ministry*

Airplanes are "air ships" and should be viewed as vessels that take us to a different place most often defined as the Church or a ministry. The definition should be aligned with what the plane is and is doing (i.e. crashing, taking-off, landing, size etc.).
Symbolizes the prophetic ministry and a fast moving ministry
Ps 48:7; 74:13-14, 1 Kings 9:26-28, Matt 8:23-27, Luke 5:4

Ps 18:10 "He mounted the cherubim and flew; he soared on the wings of the wind."

Airport - *Waiting*

A place of preparation or being matured and made ready for ministry or Kingdom work
Jer 23:22

1 Pet 3:20 "who disobeyed long ago when God waited patiently in the days of Noah while the ark was being built. In it only a few people, eight in all, were saved through water,"

Interpreting Dreams Dictionary

Alligator (also Leviathan, Crocodile & Dinosaur) - *Ancient / Concealed*
> Evil from the past, deception, ancient demonic control, beyond the strength of man to tame, warning of danger or a trap, destruction.
> *Ps 74:14, Ps 104:26, Is 27:1, Luke 13:32*
>
> *Job 41:1 "Can you pull in the leviathan with a fishhook or tie down his tongue with a rope?"*

Altar - *Sacrifice or Offering*
> Offering or sacrifice with a specific intent, Jesus, Lamb of God, worship, repentance, prayer, gratitude, self denial, change of heart
> *Gen. 33:20, 35:7, Exo 27:1, 2 Chr 4:1; 7:1,3, 2 Sam 24:18-25, Acts 17:23*
>
> *Gen 8:20 "Then Noah built an altar to the LORD and, taking some of all the clean animals and clean birds, he sacrificed burnt offerings on it."*

Anchor - *Hope*
> An assurance of hope, steadfast security, strength and steadiness in times of trial or doubt.
> *Heb 6:19*
>
> *Acts 27:13 "When a gentle south wind began to blow, they thought they had obtained what they wanted; so they weighed anchor and sailed along the shore of Crete."*

Angel(s) - *Protection or Messenger*
Protection that surrounds, God's assurance of His working with us, dispatched warrior, worshipper, messenger, ministering spirit
Ps 91:11, Heb 1:14; 13:2, Luke 1:26-38

Ps 34:7 "The angel of the LORD encamps around those who fear him, and he delivers them."

Ankles - *Weakness*
Positive - Healing, strengthening, preparation for working in ministry
Negative - Weakness, infirmity, imprisonment
Acts 3:7

Ps 105:18 "They bruised his feet with shackles, his neck was put in irons,"

Anoint - *Consecration*
Set apart, holy, divine appointment, servant, healing, spiritual vision, marked, made to stand out
Exo 40:9, Rom 3:3, Ps 23:5, Rev 3:18

Exo 28:41 "After you put these clothes on your brother Aaron and his sons, anoint and ordain them. Consecrate them so they may serve me as priests."

Interpreting Dreams Dictionary

Ant - *Industrious Team Work*
Positive - Hardworking, diligent, prepared, wise
Negative - Annoying, angry or biting words
Pro 30:25

Pro 6:6-8 " ⁶ Go to the ant, you sluggard; consider its ways and be wise! ⁷ It has no commander, no overseer or ruler, ⁸ yet it stores its provisions in summer and gathers its food at harvest."

Antelope - *Swift yet Vulnerable (similar to Deer)*
Positive - Gentle, swift, graceful, able to overcome (leap over) obstacles
Negative - Vulnerable, trapped, hunted, weak

Isa 51:20 "Your sons have fainted; they lie at the head of every street, like antelope caught in a net. They are filled with the wrath of the LORD and the rebuke of your God."

Antiques - *Generational*
Positive - Generational blessings, reflecting and recalling the past
Negative - Generational curses, reflecting and living in the past

Jer 6:16 "This is what the LORD says: "Stand at the crossroads and look; ask for the ancient paths, ask where the good way is, and walk in it, and you will find rest for your souls. But you said, 'We will not walk in it.'

Interpreting Dreams Dictionary

Apples - *Fruit of the Spirit*
 Positive - Spiritual fruit, love, prophetic word, security, completion, finished product
 Negative - Temptation, negative allure
 Gal 5:22-23, Zec 2:8, Deu 32:10, Pro 25:11

 Ps 17:8 "Keep me as the apple of your eye; hide me in the shadow of your wings"

Ark - *Security / Protection*
 Strength, deliverance, protection, place of refuge, commandments, holy, anointing, law, provision, covenant, authority
 2 Chr 6:41, Exo 25:16, 21, 33, 1 Sam 6:19, Heb 9:4, 1 Pet 3:20-21

 Num 10:33 "So they set out from the mountain of the LORD and traveled for three days. The ark of the covenant of the LORD went before them during those three days to find them a place to rest."

Arm - *Rescue*
    Positive - Strength, rescue, help, Savior
    Negative - Attacker, accusation, strike against, strong opposition, battle
    2 Kings 17:36, 2 Chr 32:8, Psa 77:15, Isa 30:32; 33:2; 59:16, Jer 32:17, Acts 13:17

    Deu 7:19 "You saw with your own eyes the great trials, the miraculous signs and wonders, the mighty hand and outstretched arm, with which the LORD your God brought you out. The LORD your God will do the same to all the peoples you now fear."

Armor - *Protection / Preparation*
    Positive - Covering worn in preparation for war, light, righteousness,
    Negative - Unprepared, darkness, pride, flesh
    1 Kings 20:11, Rom 13:12

    Eph 6:11-13 "[11]Put on the full armor of God so that you can take your stand against the devil's schemes. [12]For our struggle is not against flesh and blood, but against the rulers, against the authorities, against the powers of this dark world and against the spiritual forces of evil in the heavenly realms. [13]Therefore put on the full armor of God, so that when the day of evil comes, you may be able to stand your ground, and after you have done everything, to stand."

Army / Armies - *Warriors*
   Positive - Warring angels, Godly army, spiritual warfare, commissioned
   Negative - Demonic forces, dispatched by man, ways of the flesh, demonic attack.
   Num 20:20, Deu 20:1, Jos 5:14

   1 Chr 12:22 "Day after day men came to help David, until he had a great army, like the army of God."

Arrows - *Words*
   Positive - Prophetic words, Word of the Lord, clear direction, hitting the target
   Negative - Gossip, deceit, lies, demonic attacks, evil intentions toward another.
   Psa 11:2, Rom 5:3-4, Jer. 9:8, Psa 127:4, 2 Kings 13:17

   Pro 25:18-19 "Like a club or a sword or a sharp arrow is the man who gives false testimony against his neighbor."

Ashes - *Humbling*
   Positive - Repentance, turning from sins, consciousness of our desperate need for God
   Negative - Devastation, ruin, destruction, self-loathing
   Ps 102:9, Job 13:12; 42:6

   Exo 9:8 "Then the LORD said to Moses and Aaron, Take handfuls of soot from a furnace and have Moses toss it into the air in the presence of Pharaoh."

Atom Bomb - Massive *Power*
   Positive - Power of the Holy Spirit, outpouring, miracle-working power
   Negative - Sudden terror, sign of the last days, destruction
   Acts 1:8; 2:17, 19

   1 Thes 5:3 "While people are saying, "Peace and safety," destruction will come on them suddenly, as labor pains on a pregnant woman, and they will not escape."

Attic - *Memories*
   Positive - Positive thinking, learning, awareness of the spiritual realm
   Negative - Negative thinking, unwillingness to change, holding onto junk from the past
   Phil 3:13

   Acts 10:9-11 "⁹About noon the following day as they were on their journey and approaching the city, Peter went up on the roof to pray. ¹⁰He became hungry and wanted something to eat, and while the meal was being prepared, he fell into a trance. ¹¹He saw heaven opened and something like a large sheet being let down to earth by its four corners.

Automobile - *Church / Personal Ministry / Occupation*
　　The definition is best taken in context of what the car is and is doing (i.e. crashing, moving, standing, big, small etc.). A job is just as important as ministry - it is what God has called you to do that matters.
　　Positive - Ministry, personal life, livelihood, spiritual warfare
　　Negative - Hinderance, sickness, pride, waste, loss, strife, battles
　　2 Kings 2:11-12; 10:16; 1 Thes 2:18, Acts 8:28-38

Gen 41:43 "He had him ride in a chariot as his second in command, and men shouted before him, "Make way!" Thus he put him in charge of the whole land of Egypt."

Autumn - *Completion / Change of season*
　　Positive - Turn from sin, transformation, conclusion, a natural change of season
　　Negative - Termination, death, end
　　Jer 8:20

Isa 64:6 "All of us have become like one who is unclean, and all our righteous acts are like filthy rags; we all shrivel up like a leaf, and like the wind our sins sweep us away."

Axe - *Truth / Untruth*
> Positive - Gospel, preaching, truth, exhortation, repentance, equipped, strong
> Negative - Lies, rebuke, unrepentant, judgement
> *Ecc 10:10, Pro 27:17*
>
> *Matt 3:10 "The ax is already at the root of the trees, and every tree that does not produce good fruit will be cut down and thrown into the fire."*

-B-

Baby - *New Life / Beginning*
> Positive - Purity, Inclined toward pureness, desiring pure spiritual food
> Negative - Immature, selfish, motivated by the flesh, easily swayed
> *Jam 1:4, Heb 5:12-14*

> *1 Pet 2:2 "Like newborn babies, crave pure spiritual milk, so that by it you may grow up in your salvation,"*

Backwards - *Past*
> Positive - Returning to the past, behind, over with, casting sin behind you
> Negative - Returning to the past, backsliding, going backward, out of balance
> *Exo 33:23, Mrk 8:32-33, Phil 3:13-14, Jer 14:7*

> *1 Kings 14:9 "You have done more evil than all who lived before you. You have made for yourself other gods, idols made of metal; you have provoked me to anger and thrust me behind your back."*

Backside (Rear) - *Concealed / Behind / Past*
   Positive - End of a season, something that is over with, hidden, protected
   Negative - Concealed, something that is over with, to put out of sight
   Mark 8:32-33, Phil 3:13-14

   Josh 8:4 "with these orders: "Listen carefully. You are to set an ambush behind the city. Don't go very far from it. All of you be on the alert."

Bag(s) - *Gifts / Provision*
   Positive - Gifts of the Spirit, gift, talent, provision, redemption
   Negative - Weight, past, emotional baggage, deceit, idolatry
   Matt 25:15, Job 14:17

   Isa 46:6 "Some pour out gold from their bags and weigh out silver on the scales; they hire a goldsmith to make it into a god, and they bow down and worship it."

Bake (ing) - Worship / Cleansing
Positive - Hospitality, God's provision, worship, cleansing, an act of obedience
Negative - "In the fire", testing, trials
Gen 25:34, Lev 26:26, 23:17

Dan 3:16-18 "Shadrach, Meshach and Abednego replied to the king, "O Nebuchadnezzar, we do not need to defend ourselves before you in this matter. ¹⁷ If we are thrown into the blazing furnace, the God we serve is able to save us from it, and he will rescue us from your hand, O king. ¹⁸ But even if he does not, we want you to know, O king, that we will not serve your gods or worship the image of gold you have set up."

Bank - *Security*
Positive - Reliable, safety, saved or saving, sure, heavenly reward
Negative - Withholding, defensive, controlling
Matt 6:20

Luke 19:23 "Why then didn't you put my money on deposit, so that when I came back, I could have collected it with interest?"

Barber or Beauty Shop - *Place of Change*
    Positive: Removal of sin covenants, breaking of bad habits, preparation, holiness, transformation, wisdom
    Negative: Vanity, carnality, outward man, the occult, religious spirit
    Rom 12:2, Hos 10:5, Pro 31:30, 1 Cor. 11:15, Ps 29:2, Eze 28:12

    Jud 16:17 "So he told her everything. "No razor has ever been used on my head," he said, "because I have been a Nazirite set apart to God since birth. If my head were shaved, my strength would leave me, and I would become as weak as any other man."

Basement - *Soul / Deep Foundation*
    Positive - Refuge, solitude, retreat
    Negative - Carnal or fleshly nature, lust, discouragement or depression, things hidden and done in secret
    Psa 63:9

    Jer 38:6 "So they took Jeremiah and put him into the cistern of Malkijah, the king's son, which was in the courtyard of the guard. They lowered Jeremiah by ropes into the cistern; it had no water in it, only mud, and Jeremiah sank down into the mud."

Interpreting Dreams Dictionary

Bat - *Witchcraft*
Unclean, darkness, flighty, unstable, receiving of unclean things, accepting of trash, related most often to witchcraft and the occult
Isa 2:19-21, Lev 11:19

Deu 14:18 "the stork, any kind of heron, the hoopoe and the bat."

Bathroom - *Deliverance*
Positive - Repentance, confession, healing, cleansing,
Negative - Lust, desires of the flesh
Pro 17:14, 2 Sam 11:24, John 13:10

Isa 1:16 "wash and make yourselves clean. Take your evil deeds out of my sight! Stop doing wrong,"

Bear - *Fierce Fighter*
Positive - Strength, warrior, determined, protective
Negative - Danger, isolation, intimidation, destruction, fierce opposition
Dan 7:5, Isa 11:7, Rev 13:2, Amos 5:19, 2 Kings 2:23-24, Pro 17:12

2 Sam 17:8 "You know your father and his men; they are fighters, and as fierce as a wild bear robbed of her cubs. Besides, your father is an experienced fighter; he will not spend the night with the troops."

Beast - *Lucifer*
Something negative that opposes itself to God

Rev. 13:18 "All inhabitants of the earth will worship the beast - all whose names have not been written in the book of life belonging to the Lamb that was slain from the creation of the world."

Beating or Beaten - *Warfare*
Positive - Spiritual warfare, defend, correction
Negative - Abuse, mockery, gossip, slander, wounded, injury
Joel 3:10, I Cor 9:26 - 27, 1 Pet 2:20

Isa 2:4 "He will judge between the nations and will settle disputes for many peoples. They will beat their swords into plowshares and their spears into pruning hooks. Nation will not take up sword against nation, nor will they train for war anymore."

Beaver - *Builder*
Positive - Hard-worker, incessantly busy, clever, creative
Negative - Selfish, creating blocks to the Spirit flowing

Prov 24:3 "By wisdom a house is built, and through understanding it is established;"

Bed or Bedroom - *Intimacy / Rest*
   Positive - Salvation, meditation, intimacy, privacy, peace, covenant
   Negative - Carnal covenant, sin, adultery, lust
   Heb 13:4, Psa 139:8

   Psa 4:4 "In your anger do not sin; when you are on your beds, search your hearts and be silent. Selah"

Bees - *Gossip*
   Positive - Capable of producing sweet-tasting, desirable food, hard-working team player, follower of commands
   Negative - Stinging or biting words, surrounding, enemy, affliction
   Lev 20:24, Psa 118:12

   Deu 1:44 "The Amorites who lived in those hills came out against you; they chased you like a swarm of bees and beat you down from Seir all the way to Hormah."

Belt - *Truth*
   Positive - Truth, righteousness, upright, prepared, controlled, spiritual reproduction, holds things together
   Negative - Controlling, demise, abuse, lies
   Isa 11:5, Acts 21:11

   Eph 6:14 "Stand firm then, with the belt of truth buckled around your waist, with the breastplate of righteousness in place,"

Bind or Bound - *Healing / Covenant*
    Positive - Covenant, made whole, healing from past injury (emotional or physical)
    Negative - Sinful covenant, injury, wounded
    Pro 6:21, Isa 61:1 Matt 16:19, Psa 147:3

Isa 30:26 "The moon will shine like the sun, and the sunlight will be seven times brighter, like the light of seven full days, when the LORD binds up the bruises of his people and heals the wounds he inflicted."

Bird - *Spirit*
    Positive - Holy Spirit, messenger, sacrifice, free, provision of God
    Negative - Evil spirit, gossip, hunted, sacrificed, controlled
    Matt 6:29; 13:32; 23:37, Isa 46:11, Jam 3:7

Matt 3:16 "As soon as Jesus was baptized, he went up out of the water. At that moment heaven was opened, and he saw the Spirit of God descending like a dove and lighting on him."

Birth - *New Begining*
    Positive - New work, new ministry, fresh start, new beginning, dependent
    Negative - Trials, pain, sin, immature, dependent
    Jam 1:14-15, 1 Pet 1:3

Isa 43:19 "See, I am doing a new thing! Now it springs up; do you not perceive it? I am making a way in the desert and streams in the wasteland.

Blind - *Ignorance*
    Positive - Grace, mercy, not focused on flaws, seeking the Lord in a new way
    Negative - Spiritual blindness, unseeing, naive, religious spirit, foolish, lust, greed
    Matt 15:14; 23:16, Rev 3:18

    John 9:25 "He replied, "Whether he is a sinner or not, I don't know. One thing I do know. I was blind but now I see!"

Blood - *Life of the Father*
    Positive - Spiritual covenant, cleansing, new birth, new beginning, forgiven, mercy, life, atonement
    Negative - Sinful covenant, injury, trauma, impure
    Gen 9:6, Exo 12:13; 24:8, Lev 17:11, Matt 26:28, Rev 5:9

    Heb 9:12 "He did not enter by means of the blood of goats and calves; but he entered the Most Holy Place once for all by his own blood, having obtained eternal redemption."

Boat - *Ministry or Business*
    Local Church, ministry, personal ministry, ministry or business works in the world at large
    Judge size of ministry by size of vessel i.e. jet ski vs. cruise ship
    Psa 18:10, Acts 27:1-2, Luke 5:4

    Pro 31:14 "She is like the merchant ships, bringing her food from afar."

Interpreting Dreams Dictionary

Bones - *Spirit / Structure*
　　Positive - Eternal, heart condition, inner-strength
　　Negative - Lack of structure, death, spiritually dry
　　Matt 23:27, Pro 17:22, Psa 102:5

　　Eze 37:11 "Then he said to me: "Son of man, these bones are the whole house of Israel. They say, 'Our bones are dried up and our hope is gone; we are cut off.'"

Book - *Record / Remembrance*
　　Positive - The Word of God, witness, recall, remembrance, conscience, salvation, reward, law, memories
　　Negative - Painful memories, guilt, record of wrongdoing, accusation, law
　　2 Cor 3:2, Jos 1:8, Phil 4:3

　　Rev 20:12 "And I saw the dead, great and small, standing before the throne, and books were opened. Another book was opened, which is the book of life. The dead were judged according to what they had done as recorded in the books."

Branch(es) - *Offspring / Extensions*
 Positive - Children, disciples, students, fruit of the Spirit, connected, extension of
 Negative - Fruit of the flesh, unhealthy attachments
 Isa 4:2, Jer 33:15

John 15:5 "I am the vine; you are the branches. If a man remains in me and I in him, he will bear much fruit; apart from me you can do nothing."

Brass - *Word*
 Positive - Word of God, purification
 Negative - False word, judgment, hypocrisy, false, of inferior quality
 Rev 1:15, 1 Cor 13:1, 2 Chr 12:10

Isa 48:4 "For I knew how stubborn you were; the sinews of your neck were iron, your forehead was bronze."

Bread - *Life or Word*
 Positive - Doctrine, covenant, the church, substance, provision
 Negative - (Example rotten, stale or moldy bread) without revelation, stale, religious tradition, unfit, defiled
 Josh 9:5, Mal 1:7, Jud 7:13-14, John 13:18, 2 Thes 3:8

Matt 4:4 "Jesus answered, "It is written: 'Man does not live on bread alone, but on every word that comes from the mouth of God."

Bride - *Church*
    Positive - Covenant, ceremony, tradition
    Negative - Ungodly covenant, religious tradition
    Isa 62:5, Eph 5:31-32, 2 Cor 6:14

    Rev 19:7 "Let us rejoice and be glad and give him glory! For the wedding of the Lamb has come, and his bride has made herself ready."

Bridge - *Support / Way*
    Positive - Faith, covenant, support
    Negative - Unstable faith, ungodly covenant, lack of support
    Gen 32:22, Isa 43:2

    1 Cor 10:13 "No temptation has seized you except what is common to man. And God is faithful; He will not let you be tempted beyond what you can bear. But when you are tempted, He will also provide a way out so that you can stand up under it."

Broom - *Cleaning / Witchcraft*
    Positive - "Cleaning house", departure from sin, removal of old habits
    Negative - Curses, witchcraft
    Gal 5:19-20

    John 2:15 "So he made a whip out of cords, and drove all from the temple area, both sheep and cattle; he scattered the coins of the money changers and overturned their tables."

Interpreting Dreams Dictionary

Brother - *Self*
    Positive - Friend, self, spiritual brother, someone familiar as a brother, protection, caring, provision
    Negative - Jealousy, rivalry, adversary
    Rom 14:10, Rom 2:1, Heb 13:3, Pro 17:17, Heb 13:1

    Gen 4:9 "Then the LORD said to Cain, "Where is your brother Abel?" "I don't know," he replied. "Am I my brother's keeper?"

Bull - *Atonement*
    Positive - Atonement, sacrifice, offering
    Negative - Stubborn, accusation, opposition, sin
    Exo 29:36, Lev 4:3

    Eze 43:19 "You are to give a young bull as a sin offering to the priests, who are Levites, of the family of Zadok, who come near to minister before me, declares the Sovereign LORD."

Butter - *Works / Riches*
    Positive - Obedience, enriching or fattening affect, worker of the Word, healing, prosperity
    Negative - Disobedience, smooth talker, deceiver
    Isa 7:15, Pro 30:33

    Psa 55:21 "His speech is smooth as butter, yet war is in his heart; his words are more soothing than oil, yet they are drawn swords."

Butterfly - *Metamorphosis*
   Positive - New Creation, miraculous, potential, change, transformation, a thing of great beauty
   Negative - Fragile, temporary, flighty
   2 Cor. 5:17, Joel 1:4

   Rom 12:2 "Do not conform any longer to the pattern of this world, but be transformed by the renewing of your mind. Then you will be able to test and approve what God's will is—his good, pleasing and perfect will."

-C-

Cafeteria - *Service*
Positive - Church, servant's heart, teaching, a place of study, a school, ministry of helps
Negative - Hungry, in need

Matt 25:35 "For I was hungry and you gave me something to eat, I was thirsty and you gave me something to drink, I was a stranger and you invited me in,"

Calendar - *Time*
Positive - Divine appointment, particular date or event, a plan of God
Negative - Out of God's timing, control

Hos 6:11 "'Also for you, Judah, a harvest is appointed. "Whenever I would restore the fortunes of my people,"

Calf - *Increase / Sacrifice*
Positive - Prosperity, children of God, the potential for great strength, Kingdom worker
Negative - Idolatry, false sacrifice or worship, stubbornness, rebellion, backsliding spirit

Jer 7:8-11, Hos 10:5, Mal 4:2, Hos 4:16, Exo 32:4, 35, Col 3:5

Luke 15:23 "Bring the fattened calf and kill it. Let's have a feast and celebrate."

Interpreting Dreams Dictionary

Camel - *Endurance*
 Positive - Vehicle of significant nature, specific ministry or business, strength, long journey
 Negative - Holding things in, ungraceful, ungainly, large burden
 Heb 6:15, Matt 19:24; 23:24

Mark 1:6 "John wore clothing made of camel's hair, with a leather belt around his waist, and he ate locusts and wild honey."

Car - *See Automobile*

Cards - *Facts*
 Positive - Honesty, truth, clever engineering
 Negative - Dishonesty, underhanded, unstable

Rom 12:17 "Do not repay anyone evil for evil. Be careful to do what is right in the eyes of everybody."

Carnival - *Worldly*
 Positive - Celebration, party, detached from the world, multiple talents and goods
 Negative - Carnal, exhibitionism, divination, competition
 Luke 21:34

Acts 16:16 "Once when we were going to the place of prayer, we were met by a slave girl who had a spirit by which she predicted the future. She earned a great deal of money for her owners by fortune-telling."

Carpenter - *Builder*
> Positive - Preacher, evangelist, skilled laborer, representative of Christ
> Negative - Works of the flesh
> 2 Kin 22:6, Isa 41:7, Mark 6:3

> *Matt 13:55 "'Isn't this the carpenter's son? Isn't his mother's name Mary, and aren't his brothers James, Joseph, Simon and Judas?"*

Cat - *Self-willed*
> Positive - Personal pet i.e. something precious, spirit of independence, talented hunter
> Negative - Unteachable, predator, unclean spirit, sneaky, deception, self-pity

> *Pro 7:10-12 " [10] Then out came a woman to meet him, dressed like a prostitute and with crafty intent.[11] (She is loud and defiant, her feet never stay at home;[12] now in the street, now in the squares, at every corner she lurks.)"*

Chair - *Rest / Position*
> Positive - Quiet, peace, person in or position of authority, promotion
> Negative - Out of order, unrest
> Isa 30:15, Matt 23:6

> *Col 3:1 "Since, then, you have been raised with Christ, set your hearts on things above, where Christ is seated at the right hand of God."*

Check - *Faith / Provision*
> Positive - Promise, assurance of what is to come, trust, faith, Kingdom finance, supply
> Negative - Fraud, faithlessness, deception, hypocrisy
> *Heb 11:1, Mark 4:40, Luke 17:5*

Phi 4:19 "And my God will meet all your needs according to His glorious riches in Christ Jesus."

Cheese - *Works / Blessing*
> Positive - Obedient works, provision
> Negative - Works of the flesh, rebellion
> *1 Pet 2:2, John 4:34, Job 10:10*

2 Sam 17:29 "honey and curds, sheep, and cheese from cows' milk for David and his people to eat. For they said, "The people have become hungry and tired and thirsty in the desert."

Chew(ing) - *Meditate / Judge*
> Positive - Wisdom and understanding, spirit of discernment, assessment, maturity
> Negative - Difficult truth, hesitation, judgement
> *1 Tim 4:15, Ps 49:3, Pro 24:9, Heb 5:14, 1 Cor 2:6*

Jos 1:8 "Do not let this Book of the Law depart from your mouth; meditate on it day and night, so that you may be careful to do everything written in it. Then you will be prosperous and successful."

Chicken - *Fear*
> Positive - Sustenance or provision
> Negative - Cowardly, fearful, prideful boasting, gossip, flattery, denial
> *Deu 1:29, Luke 13:34*
>
> *Luke 22:33-34 "33But he replied, "Lord, I am ready to go with you to prison and to death." 34Jesus answered, "I tell you, Peter, before the rooster crows today, you will deny three times that you know me."*

Choking - *Hindrance*
> Difficulty receiving, blocked, deterred, unfruitful, stumbling
> *Mark 4:19*
>
> *Matt 13:22 "The one who received the seed that fell among the thorns is the man who hears the word, but the worries of this life and the deceitfulness of wealth choke it, making it unfruitful."*

Christmas - *Gift*
> Positive - Festive rejoicing, celebration, spiritual gifts, good tidings
> Negative - Merchandising, worldly attitude, greed
> *Luke 11:13, 1 Cor 14:1*
>
> *Pro 18:16 "A gift opens the way for the giver and ushers him into the presence of the great."*

Church Service - *Worship*
>Positive - Worship, communion, relationship with the Father, gathering of the saints, working for God
>Negative - False worship, religious spirit
>John 4:24, Mark 7:7

Matt 13:54 "Coming to his hometown, he began teaching the people in their synagogue, and they were amazed. "Where did this man get this wisdom and these miraculous powers?" they asked."

City - *Reputation / Character (i.e. what that city is known for)*
>Positive - Protection, integrity, strength, action, provision etc.
>Negative - Immorality, stronghold, corruption, poverty etc.
>Eze 16:49-50, Jude 1:7, Acts 20:23

Pro 25:28 "Like a city whose walls are broken down is a man who lacks self-control."

Closet - *Inner Place*
>Positive - Personal, private, prayer, sanctuary
>Negative - Hidden, undisclosed, secret sin
>Matt 6:6, Luke 8:17

Luke 12:2 "There is nothing concealed that will not be disclosed, or hidden that will not be made known."

Interpreting Dreams Dictionary

Clothing - *Covering / Status*
    Positive - Righteousness, spirit, anointing, authority, protection, identity
    Negative - i.e. dirty clothing, self-righteousness, pride, unclean, legalism
    Rom 13:14, James 2:2

    Isa 64:6 "All of us have become like one who is unclean, and all our righteous acts are like filthy rags; we all shrivel up like a leaf, and like the wind our sins sweep us away."

Clouds - *Change / Promise*
    Positive - Glory, revival, good change, protection
    Negative - Trouble, distress, storm
    Zeph 1:15, Zech 10:1, Exo 14:19

    Matt 24:30 "At that time the sign of the Son of Man will appear in the sky, and all the nations of the earth will mourn. They will see the Son of Man coming on the clouds of the sky, with power and great glory."

Clown - *Fool*
    Positive - Childlike faith
    Negative - Immature, foolishness, works of the flesh, mischief
    Ecc 7:4. Pro 10:23

    Pro 12:15 "The way of a fool seems right to him, but a wise man listens to advice."

Interpreting Dreams Dictionary

Courthouse - *Judgment / Closure*
    Positive - Justice, absolution, redemption
    Negative - Judgment, persecution, difficulty, trial
    Deu 17:6-13, Psa 94:20, 1 Cor 6:1

    Exo 18:16 "Whenever they have a dispute, it is brought to me, and I decide between the parties and inform them of God's decrees and laws."

Crow / Raven - *Confusion*
    Positive - Peculiar provision, direct path
    Negative - Strife, hateful, darkness, harsh or outspoken person
    James 3:16, Isa 34:11, Psa 35:26, Pro 30:17

    1 Kings 17:4, 6 "⁴ You will drink from the brook, and I have ordered the ravens to feed you there." "⁶ The ravens brought him bread and meat in the morning and bread and meat in the evening, and he drank from the brook."

Crown - *Authority / Reward*
    Glory, honor, promotion
    2 Kings 11:12, 1 Pet 5:4

    Isa 62:3 "You will be a crown of splendor in the LORD's hand, a royal diadem in the hand of your God."

-D-

Dam - *Power*
> Positive - Source of great power, potential, provision in reserve
> Negative - Restricted or held back, hindered
> Josh 3:16

> *Psa 32:6 "Therefore let everyone who is godly pray to you while you may be found; surely when the mighty waters rise, they will not reach him."*

Dancing - *Worship / Celebration*
> Positive - Prophecy, romance, extreme happiness
> Negative - False prophecy, seduction, lust
> Exo 32:19, Matt 14:6, Lam 5:15

> *1 Sam 18:6 "When the men were returning home after David had killed the Philistine, the women came out from all the towns of Israel to meet King Saul with singing and dancing, with joyful songs and with tambourines and lutes."*

Interpreting Dreams Dictionary

Death - *Separation / Beginning*
    Positive - Repentance, dying to self, new life, the end of what was and the beginning of what is new
    Negative - Loss, sorrow, termination
    John 12:24, Heb 2:14, Isa 26:14

1 Cor 15:54 "When the perishable has been clothed with the imperishable, and the mortal with immortality, then the saying that is written will come true: "Death has been swallowed up in victory."

Daughter - *Holy Spirit*
    Positive - Spiritual daughter, spirit of God, healing ministry, worship, works of the Holy Spirit, spiritual giftings
    Negative - Manipulation, false prophet, ministry out of order
    Psa 9:14, Zec 2:10, Mat 15:22

Isa 62:11 "The LORD has made proclamation to the ends of the earth: "Say to the Daughter of Zion, 'See, your Savior comes! See, his reward is with him, and his recompense accompanies him.'"

Deer - *Graceful / Longing*
   Positive - Graceful, swift, pursuit of God, symbolic of our walk with the Lord, dependence on the Lord
   Negative - Timid, withdrawn, frightened, dependence on man
   2 Sam 22:34, Ps 42:1

   Hab 3:19 "The Sovereign LORD is my strength; He makes my feet like the feet of a deer, He enables me to go on the heights. For the director of music. On my stringed instruments."

Desert - *Barrenness*
   Positive - Withdraw, meditation, protection, place of preparation and birthing
   Negative - Unproductive, disobedience, spiritual wasteland, dryness, testing
   Psa 107:4-5, Deu 32:10

   Isa 43:19 "See, I am doing a new thing! Now it springs up; do you not perceive it? I am making a way in the desert and streams in the wasteland."

Interpreting Dreams Dictionary

Diamond - *Hard*
> Positive - Spiritual gift, precious, of great value, changeless
> Negative - Unchanging, ongoing bad habit, of no value, hardhearted
> *Eze 3:8-9, Pro 17:8, Eze 28:13*

> *Jer 17:1 "The sin of Judah is written with a pen of iron; With the point of a diamond it is engraved on the tablet of their heart, and on the horns of your altars," (NKJV)*

Doctor - *Healing / Repairing*
> Positive - Medical Doctor, restoration, spirit of Christ
> Negative - Illness
> *Mark 2:17; 5:26, 2 Chr 16:12*

> *Luke 4:23 "Jesus said to them, "Surely you will quote this proverb to me: Physician, heal yourself! Do here in your hometown what we have heard that you did in Capernaum.' "*

Interpreting Dreams Dictionary

Dog - *Strife / Backsliding Spirit*
   Positive - Friend, something held dear
   Negative - Offensive, unclean spirit, evil pursuit, gossip, outside of the Kingdom, unbeliever
   Gal 5:15, 2 Tim 3:2-4, Rev 22:15, Matt 15:26

   Pro 26:11 "As a dog returns to its vomit, so a fool repeats his folly."

Donkey - *Stubborn*
   Positive - Strength, tenacity, endurance
   Negative - Annoying, self-willed, unyielding, challenging personality
   Pro 26:3, Num 22:25, 2 Pet 2:16

   John 12:15 "'Do not be afraid, O Daughter of Zion; see, your king is coming, seated on a donkey's colt."

Door - *Entrance / Beginning*
   Positive - Christ, new opportunity, transition, challenge for us to follow, endurance
   Negative - Closed door, hindrance, blockage
   John 10:7, 9, Ps 141:3, Col 4:3

   Rev 3:8 "I know your deed. See, I have placed before you an open door that no one can shut. I know that you have little strength, yet you have kept my word and hove not denied my name

Drowning - *Overcome*
>Positive - Overtaken by the Holy Spirit, new life, dying to self in the glory of God
>Negative - Depression, grief, sadness, "drowning in debt"
>*1 Tim 6:9, Isa 61:3*
>
>*SS 8:7 "Many waters cannot quench love, Nor can the floods drown it. If a man would give for love all the wealth of his house, It would be utterly despised."*

Drugs / Drunk - *Influenced*
>Positive - Holy Spirit anointing, God's healing and sedation
>Negative - Controlled, dependency, addicted, weakness, rebellious
>*Eph 5:18, Luke 21:34, Pro 14:16, 2 Cor 4:2, Hos 4:18*
>
>*Isa 29:9 "Be stunned and amazed, blind yourselves and be sightless; be drunk, but not from wine, stagger, but not from beer."*

Interpreting Dreams Dictionary

-E-

Eagle - *Prophet / Prophetic Ministry*
Positive - Leader, prophecy, prophetic minister, nation of America
Negative - Sorcerer, predator
Exo 19:4, Isa 46:11, Job 39:27

Ps 103:5 "who satisfies your desires with good things so that your youth is renewed like the eagle's."

East - *Beginning / Start*
Positive - New day, first, new beginning, anticipation
Negative - False religion, false start
Gen 11:2, Exo 10:13

Matt 24:27 "For as lightning that comes from the east is visible even in the west, so will be the coming of the Son of Man."

Egg - *Promise / New Life*
Positive - Promise, salvation, potential, revelation
Negative - Fragile, broken promise, bad idea, without promise
Job 6:6

Luke 11:12 "Or if he asks for an egg, will give him a scorpion?"

Electricity - *Power*
> Positive - Holy Spirit, spiritual power, power source
> Negative - Witchcraft, offense, anger, powerless
> *1 Cor 4:20, Acts 1:8*
>
> *2 Thes 2:9 "The coming of the lawless one will be in accordance with the work of Satan displayed in all kinds of counterfeit miracles, signs and wonders,"*

Elephant - *Powerful*
> Positive - Large, thick-skinned, strength, great power, faithful to the herd, protective of young
> Negative - Trampled, overpowering, overbearing
> *Rom 8:37*
>
> *Phil 4:13 "I can do everything through him who gives me strength."*

Interpreting Dreams Dictionary

Elevator - *Changing Position / God's Promotion*
    Positive - Lifting up, exalting, entering the spirit realm
    Negative - Bringing down, resisting, trial, backsliding
    Pro 3:35, 1 Pet 5:5

    Rev 4:1 "After this I looked, and there before me was a door standing open in heaven. And the voice I had first heard speaking to me like a trumpet said, "Come up here, and I will show you what must take place after this."

Employer - *Authority / Provider*
    Positive - Position of authority, pastor, Christ
    Negative - Satan, evil ruler, task master
    Col 4:1, Gen 39:20, Isa 19:4

    Matt 18:27 "The servant's master took pity on him, canceled the debt and let him go."

Explosion - *Sudden*
    Positive - Swift, sudden change, increase
    Negative - Decrease, destruction
    Isa 48:3

    2 Chr 29:36 "Hezekiah and all the people rejoiced at what God had brought about for his people, because it was done so quickly."

Eyes - *Windows of Your Heart / Desire*
  Positive - Passion, revelation, deep desire, discerning
  Negative - Haughty, arrogant, lust, unbelief
  Pro 23:5, Eph 1:18, Luke 11:34

  Deu 3:21 "At that time I commanded Joshua: "You have seen with your own eyes all that the LORD your God has done to these two kings. The LORD will do the same to all the kingdoms over there where you are going."

-F-

Factory - *Production / Team Work*
Positive - Productive, motivated, working for the Kingdom, unity
Negative - The "world", materialism, lazy, idle
Rom 12:11, Luke 2:49

Jos 5:11 *"The day after the Passover, that very day, they ate some of the produce of the land: unleavened bread and roasted grain."*

Farmer - *Laborer / God*
Positive - Pastor, minister, Kingdom worker
Negative - Works of the flesh, false god
The farm itself is representative of a particular ministry or area of Kingdom work
John 15:1, Mark 4:14, 2 Cor 9:10

Jas 5:7 *"Be patient, then, brothers, until the Lord's coming. See how the farmer waits for the land to yield its valuable crop and how patient he is for the autumn and spring rains."*

Father - *Authority / Provider*
Positive - God, origin, source, reproduction, inheritance, likeness
Negative - Satan, legalism, generational curse
Eph 6:2, John 8:44

Mal 2:10 *"Have we not all one Father[a]? Did not one God create us? Why do we profane the covenant of our fathers by breaking faith with one another?"*

Father-in-Law - *Legal*
> Positive - Authoritative relationship based in law (i.e. church government or employment)
> Negative - Difficult or problem relationship, legalism, judgement
> *Exo 18:2*
>
> *John 18:13 "and brought him first to Annas, who was the father-in-law of Caiaphas, the high priest that year."*

Fish - *Spirit or Soul / People of the World*
> Positive - Mission field, souls of men, character, Holy Spirit, motivations
> Negative - Evil character, self-motivation, unclean spirit
> *Matt 13:47-48, Luke 11:11*
>
> *John 21:6 "He said, 'Throw your net on the right side of the boat and you will find some." When they did, they were unable to haul the net in because of the large number of fish."*

Flea - *Insignificant*
> Annoyance, disturbance, irritation, evasion, activity of many small demons or spirits
> *1 Sam 24:14, SS 2:15*
>
> *1 Sam 26:20 "Now do not let my blood fall to the ground far from the presence of the LORD. The king of Israel has come out to look for a flea—as one hunts a partridge in the mountains."*

Interpreting Dreams Dictionary

Fly - *Nuisance / Pestulance*
    Corruption, disease, unclean, demon, curse, ruin
    Ecc 10:1

    Exo 8:24 "And the LORD did this. Dense swarms of flies poured into Pharaoh's palace and into the houses of his officials, and throughout Egypt the land was ruined by the flies."

Foundation - *Underlying Basis*
    Positive - Founding ministry of a church, establishment, stability, prepared, the gospel, doctrine
    Negative - Unprepared, unstable, evil government
    Luke 14:29, Eph 2:20, Psa 11:3

    Psa 89:14 "Righteousness and justice are the foundation of your throne; love and faithfulness go before you."

Fox - *Subtlety*
    Cunning, stealthy, deception, evil leader, hidden sin, destruction
    S of Sol 2:15, Eze 13:4, 6

    Luke 13:32 "He replied, "Go tell that fox, 'I will drive out demons and heal people today and tomorrow, and on the third day I will reach my goal.'"

Frog - *Spirit / False Prophecy*
   Accursed, witchcraft, manipulation, prideful
   Exo 8:2-6, Psa 78:45

   Rev 16:13 "Then I saw three impure spirits that looked like frogs; they came out of the mouth of the dragon, out of the mouth of the beast and out of the mouth of the false prophet."

Front - *Future / Correct Side*
   Positive - Foretelling prophecy, immediate or far off
   Negative - Exposed sin, brought out into the open
   Gen 6:11, Rev 1:19

   2 Pet 3:14 "So then, dear friends, since you are looking forward to this, make every effort to be found spotless, blameless and at peace with him."

-G-

Giant - *Challenge*
Positive - Champion, strength, overcomer
Negative - Spiritual warfare, insurmountable challenge, obstacle, fruit of the flesh
Num 13:32-33, 2 Chr 20:6

2 Sam 21:20 "In still another battle, which took place at Gath, there was a huge man with six fingers on each hand and six toes on each foot—twenty-four in all. He also was descended from Rapha."

Goat - *Sin / False Sheep*
Positive - Sacrifice, celebration
Negative - Strife, unbelieving, rebellious, stubborn, argumentative
Lev 16:10, Matt 25:33

Num 28:22 "Include one male goat as a sin offering to make atonement for you."

Gold - *Wisdom / Glory / Wealth*
Positive - Glory of God, truth, refined faith, righteousness
Negative - Self-glorification, irreverence, blasphemy
Jam 2:2-4, 2 Chr 16:2

Exo 25:11 "Overlay it with pure gold, both inside and out, and make a gold molding around it."

Governor - *Ruler / Authority*
    Positive - Christ, leader, authority
    Negative - Evil leader, Satan, dictator
    Mal 1:8, Acts 23: 24, 26; Jer 30:21

    Isa 9:6 "For to us a child is born, to us a son is given, and the government will be on his shoulders. And he will be called Wonderful Counselor, Mighty God, Everlasting Father, Prince of Peace."

Grandchild - *Heir / Ministry*
    Positive - Blessings inherited, spiritual heritage, family virtue, consequence of something or someone that we have ministered to
    Negative - Generational curse, iniquity
    2 Tim 1:5, 2 Kings 17:41

    Exo 34:7 "maintaining love to thousands, and forgiving wickedness, rebellion and sin. Yet he does not leave the guilty unpunished; he punishes the children and their children for the sin of the fathers to the third and fourth generation."

Grandparent - *Past*
    Positive - Spiritual inheritance, wisdom, spiritual legacy, spiritual identity
    Negative - Generational sins, unrighteous or evil spiritual inheritance
    Pro 13:22

    2 Tim 1:5 "I have been reminded of your sincere faith, which first lived in your grandmother Lois and in your mother Eunice and, I am persuaded, now lives in you also."

Grapes - *Fruit / Victory*
   Positive - Fruit of the Spirit, word of God, promise, great provision
   Negative - Fruit of the flesh, wrath
   Matt 20:16, Rev 14:18

   Gen 40:10-11 "and on the vine were three branches. As soon as it budded, it blossomed, and its clusters ripened into grapes. 11 Pharaoh's cup was in my hand, and I took the grapes, squeezed them into Pharaoh's cup and put the cup in his hand.""

Groom - *Christ / Covenant*
   Marriage, spiritual leader, headship, spiritual authority
   John 3:29, Eze 16:8-14

   Psa 19:5 "which is like a bridegroom coming forth from his pavilion, like a champion rejoicing to run his course."

Gun - *Warfare / Words*
   Positive - Spiritual authority, word of God, spiritual warfare
   Negative - Words that wound, gossip, accusation, spiritual warfare
   Luke 11:21-22, Acts 19:13, 15-116

   Ps 64:4 "They shoot from ambush at the innocent man; they shoot at him suddenly, without fear."

- H -

Hail - *Judgement / False Blessing*
   Positive - Discernment, cleansing, repentance
   Negative - Punishment, destruction, a blessing out of season, onslaught
   Isa 28:17, Hag 2:17

   Exo 9:19 "Give an order now to bring your livestock and everything you have in the field to a place of shelter, because the hail will fall on every man and animal that has not been brought in and is still out in the field, and they will die.'"

Hair - *Covering / Glory of God*
   Positive - Covenant, spiritual authority, order, tradition, beauty of heart
   Negative - Evil covenant, sinful nature, evil doctrine
   Jud 16:17, Num 8:7, 1 Cor 11:6

   1 Cor 11:15 "but that if a woman has long hair, it is her glory? For long hair is given to her as a covering."

Hammer - *Force / Power*
    Positive - Word of God, powerful preaching, building
    Negative - Gossip, hurtful words, destruction
    Jer 23:29, Pro 25:18

    Isa 41:7 "The craftsman encourages the goldsmith, and he who smooths with the hammer spurs on him who strikes the anvil. He says of the welding, "It is good." He nails down the idol so it will not topple."

Hawk - *Predator*
    Positive - Intercessor, warrior
    Negative - Sorcerer, evil spirit, enemy
    Acts 20:30, Gen 10:9

    Job 39:26 "Does the hawk take flight by your wisdom and spread his wings toward the south?"

Horse - *Ministry / Career / Work*
    Positive - Building the Kingdom, strength, spiritual warfare, tradition, ushering in
    Negative - Works of the flesh, burdened, old-fashioned or traditional way of doing things
    Jer 5:8, Psa 33:17, Rev 6:1-8

    Rev 19:11 "I saw heaven standing open and there before me was a white horse, whose rider is called Faithful and True. With justice he judges and makes war."

Interpreting Dreams Dictionary

Hospital - *Healing / Restoration*
    Positive - Place of healing, Church, ministry
    Negative - Wounds, discouragement, illness
    Ps a109:22, Luke 10:30; 33-34

    Isa 53:5 "But he was pierced for our transgressions, he was crushed for our iniquities; the punishment that brought us peace was upon him, and by his wounds we are healed."

Hotel - *Rest / Business*
    Positive - Rest, peace, tranquility, travel, temporary home
    Negative - Restless, lonely, detached, temporary home
    Acts 28:15

    Psa 119:54 "Your decrees are the theme of my song wherever I lodge."

House - *Church / Workplace / Family*
    Positive - House of God, roots, place of security
    Negative - Church out of order, dysfunction, abuse
    Acts 16:31, 1 Chr 17:5, John 14:1-4

    Mark 13:34-35 "34It's like a man going away: He leaves his house and puts his servants in charge, each with his assigned task, and tells the one at the door to keep watch. 35"Therefore keep watch because you do not know when the owner of the house will come back—whether in the evening, or at midnight, or when the rooster crows, or at dawn."

Husband - *Authority*
>   Positive - God or Jesus, pastor, spiritual leader or authority
>   Negative - Abuse, control, ineffective leader
>   *Isa 54:5, Jer 3:20*
>
>   *1 Cor 7:4 "The wife's body does not belong to her alone but also to her husband. In the same way, the husband's body does not belong to him alone but also to his wife."*

Interpreting Dreams Dictionary

- I -

Ice / Snow - *Words / Blessing*
    Positive - Pure blessing, grace, saturated, covered
    Negative - Harsh words, dangerous, unsure footing, slipping
    Isa 55:10, Job 16:3-4

    Psa 73:2 "But as for me, my feet had almost slipped; I had nearly lost my foothold."

Incense - *Worship*
    Positive - Prayer, worship, praise, service to God, effectiveness of your prayer life
    Negative - Idolatry, service out of wrong motive, self-glorification
    Psa 141:2, Isa 60:6, Luke 1:10-11

    Jer 1:16 "I will pronounce my judgments on my people because of their wickedness in forsaking me, in burning incense to other gods and in worshiping what their hands have made."

Indian - *Origins*
    Positive - Firstborn, leader, native, mission field
    Negative - Flesh, savage, foreigner, threat
    Col 3:9, Acts 15:22

    Gen 49:3 "Reuben, you are my firstborn, my might, the first sign of my strength, excelling in honor, excelling in power."

Insurance - *Faith / Promise*
  Positive - Guarantee, prepared, covering, confidence, promise of future provision
  Negative - Exposed, unprepared, wavering
  2 Sam 22:3

  Heb 10:22 "let us draw near to God with a sincere heart in full assurance of faith, having our hearts sprinkled to cleanse us from a guilty conscience and having our bodies washed with pure water."

Iron - *Strength / Challenge*
  Positive - Powerful, correction, indestructible
  Negative - Stronghold, offense
  Dan 2:40, Isa 48:4, Deu 28:48

  Rev 2:27 "He will rule them with an iron scepter; he will dash them to pieces like pottery'"

Ironing - *Bringing to Order*
  Positive - Change, preparation, encouragement, righteous instruction, repentance, reconciliation
  Negative - Under pressure, unyielding, stiff
  Eph 5:27, 2 Cor 1:8

  Phi 3:14 "I press on toward the goal to win the prize for which God has called me heavenward in Christ Jesus."

-J-

Jacket – *Covering*
> Positive - Condition of life, anointing, authority, protection, identification, praise
> Negative - Grief, heaviness, shameful ways, confusion
> *Exo 28:42, Deu 24:13; 10:18*
>
> *1 Sam 18:4 "Jonathan took off the robe he was wearing and gave it to David, along with his tunic, and even his sword, his bow and his belt."*

Jacuzzi - *Cleansing / Restoration*
> Positive - Sanctification, repentance, rejuvenation, healing
> Negative - Temptation, "in hot water", trouble
> *Psa 51:2-3, Eph 5:25-26*
>
> *2 Sam 11:2 "One evening David got up from his bed and walked around on the roof of the palace. From the roof he saw a woman bathing. The woman was very beautiful,"*

Interpreting Dreams Dictionary

Jaguar (also cat, cheetah, leopard, tiger) – *Crafty*
    Positive - Strong, agile, "landing on your feet", success, stealth warrior
    Negative - Unclean spirit, mysterious, laying in wait, crafty, stealth warrior
    1Pet 1: 24, Ps. 37:2, Jer. 5:6

    Jer 13:23 "Can the Ethiopian change his skin or the leopard its spots? Neither can you do good who are accustomed to doing evil."

Jail – *Bondage / Mindsets*
    Rebellion, unforgiveness, captivity, serious trouble, addiction, lost souls, torment
    Luke 4:18, Heb 2:15, 2 Tim 2:25-26

    Jer 38:6 "So they took Jeremiah and put him into the cistern of Malkijah, the king's son, which was in the courtyard of the guard. They lowered Jeremiah by ropes into the cistern; it had no water in it, only mud, and Jeremiah sank down into the mud."

Jet – *See Airplane*

Jet ski – *See Boat*

Jewelry - *Treasure / Victory*
: Positive - Precious, God's gifts, truth, achievement, self-worth
: Negative - Idolatry, self-glorification, pride, loss of self-worth, mockery, plunder
: *Pro 17:8, Jam 2:2, 2 Tim 4:3*

> *Gen 24:53 "Then the servant brought out gold and silver jewelry and articles of clothing and gave them to Rebekah; he also gave costly gifts to her brother and to her mother."*

Judge - *Authority / Discernment*
: Positive - God, conscience, Jesus, discernment
: Negative - Evil authority, judgmental, critical spirit, Satan
: *Acts 17:31, Exo 18:21-23, 1 Cor 2:14*

> *Ezra 7:25 "And you, Ezra, in accordance with the wisdom of your God, which you possess, appoint magistrates and judges to administer justice to all the people of Trans-Euphrates—all who know the laws of your God. And you are to teach any who do not know them."*

-K-

Keys – *Revelation*
> Access, authority, wisdom, prophetic revelation, understanding, indispensable, Christ
> Matt 16:19, Luke 11:52, Exo 31:3

> *Rev 1:18 "I am the Living One; I was dead, and behold I am alive for ever and ever! And I hold the keys of death and Hades."*

Kindergarten – *See School*

Kiss – *Agreement*
> Positive - Covenant, affirmation, greeting, acceptance, reconciliation, gratitude, identification, blessings
> Negative - Betrayal, allurement, seduction, temptation, deception
> Luke 7:36-50, 1 Kin 19:18, Hos 13:2, 2 Sam 20:9, Acts 20:37

> *Luke 15:20 "So he got up and went to his father. "But while he was still a long way off, his father saw him and was filled with compassion for him; he ran to his son, threw his arms around him and kissed him."*

Interpreting Dreams Dictionary

Kitchen – *Preparation*
    Positive - Heart's desire, plans, motives, passion, place of separation to the Lord
    Negative - Selfish ambition, affliction, "in the fire", trials
    Heb 4:12, 1 Cor 11:24

    Hos 7:6 "Their hearts are like an oven; they approach him with intrigue. Their passion smolders all night; in the morning it blazes like a flaming fire.

Knee or Kneeling - *Submission*
    Positive - (right knee) Respect, worship, obedience, recognition of authority, humbling of heart
    Negative - (left knee) Idolatry, stubbornness, unyielding, weakness
    Rom 14:11, Isa 45:23, Heb 12:12

    Php 2:10 "that at the name of Jesus every knee should bow, in heaven and on earth and under the earth,"

Knife - *Words*
    Positive - Revelation, truth, words that pierce the heart
    Negative - Sharp rebuke, angry words, gossip, accusation
    Psa 52:2

    Tit 1:13 "This testimony is true. Therefore, rebuke them sharply, so that they will be sound in the faith"

Interpreting Dreams Dictionary

-L-

Ladder - *Task Oriented Ascending / Descending*
  Positive - Enable, escape, promotion, rescue or help
  Negative - Struggle, demotion, abandonment
  John 3:13

  Gen 28:12-13 "He had a dream in which he saw a stairway resting on the earth, with its top reaching to heaven, and the angels of God were ascending and descending on it. 13 There above it stood the LORD, and he said: "I am the LORD, the God of your father Abraham and the God of Isaac. I will give you and your descendants the land on which you are lying."

Lame – *Weak / Not Completely Fruitful*
  Positive - Healing, dependent
  Negative - Imperfect, needy, inconsistent, rendered impotent, unfulfilled
  Lev 21:18, Job 29:15

  Luke 7:22 "So he replied to the messengers, "Go back and report to John what you have seen and heard: The blind receive sight, the lame walk, those who have leprosy are cured, the deaf hear, the dead are raised, and the good news is preached to the poor."

Lead – *Weighty*
  Positive - Refining, supportive, discernment
  Negative - Burden, judgement, foolishness
  Jer 6:27, Job 19:24, Amos 7:7-8, Zech 5:7-8

  Exod 15:10 "But you blew with your breath, and the sea covered them. They sank like lead in the mighty waters."

Leaves - *Words of Life*
   Positive - Covering, covenant, testimony, spiritual doctrine, healing
   Negative - Broken covenant, self-justification, shame, temporary, ill-health
   Matt 21:19, Isa 64:6, Gen 3:7

   Rev 22:2 "down the middle of the great street of the city. On each side of the river stood the tree of life, bearing twelve crops of fruit, yielding its fruit every month. And the leaves of the tree are for the healing of the nations."

Legs – *Support / Ability*
   Positive - Spirit, strength, equipped to do a task
   Negative - Broken spirit, not supported, weakness, ill-equipped
   Lev 7:32-34, Isa 47:2

   Pro 26:7 "Like a lame man's legs that hang limp is a proverb in the mouth of a fool."

Leopard - *See Jaguar*

Interpreting Dreams Dictionary

Library – *Knowledge / Resource*
    Positive - wisdom, education, learning, research, receiving of information
    Negative - distraction (i.e. noisy library), lack of resources
    James 3:13-15, 1Cor 8:1, Rom 2:20

    2 Tim 2:15 "Do your best to present yourself to God as one approved, a workman who does not need to be ashamed and who correctly handles the word of truth."

Lice – *Conviction*
    Positive - Deliverance from a spirit of guilt or shame
    Negative - Accusation, affliction, guilt, shame, evil influence
    Exo 8:16-18

    Psa 105:31 "He spoke, and there came swarms of flies, And lice in all their territory." (NKJV)

Lightning - *Power / Illumination*
    Positive - Instantaneous miracle, revelational knowledge, ability to see
    Negative - Judgment, accusation, destructive force
    Psa 144:6, Luke 10:17-18

    Matt 28:3 "His appearance was like lightning, and his clothes were white as snow."

Interpreting Dreams Dictionary

Lion – *Dominion / Victory*
Positive - Christ, King, bravery, powerful, daring, victorious
Negative - Satan, spirit of legalism, destruction
Jud 14:18, Pro 30:30, Pro 28:1

1 Pet 5:8 "Be self-controlled and alert. Your enemy the devil prowls around like a roaring lion looking for someone to devour."

Lips – *Words*
Positive - That which gives us the ability to speak, offers of prayer, praise or worship, producing spiritual fruit
Negative - Accusation, temptation, seduction, slander, no confidence to speak, over-confidence
Heb 13:15, Pro 7:21, Pro 10:19, Psa 63:5

Psa 119:13 "With my lips I recount all the laws that come from your mouth."

Living room - *Revealed / Social*
Positive - Fellowship, out in the open, truth exposed, transparent, honest
Negative - Dysfunctional relationships, hypocrisy, untruth
Mark 2:4-5

Mark 5:19 "Jesus did not let him, but said, "Go home to your family and tell them how much the Lord has done for you, and how he has had mercy on you."

-M-

Machine - *Work or Motion / Success*
Positive - Productivity, in motion, making things happen, a role to play, unity
Negative - Idle works, idle words, stagnant
Ecc 7:29, Rom 7:5, Matt 12:36

Pro 18:20 "From the fruit of his mouth a man's stomach is filled; with the harvest from his lips he is satisfied."

Man - *Messenger / Model of Character*
Positive - Angel, messenger from God, Jesus, divine or natural helper
Negative - Demon, evil resolve, destroyer
Heb 13:2, Luke 10:33

Matt 2:13 "When they had gone, an angel of the Lord appeared to Joseph in a dream. "Get up," he said, "take the child and his mother and escape to Egypt. Stay there until I tell you, for Herod is going to search for the child to kill him."

Marriage - *Covenant / Mystery*
Positive - Bride of Christ, entwined, woven together, agreement, sacred
Negative - Separated, evil covenant
Rev 2:12, Neh 13:27

Eph 5:31-32 "31'For this reason a man will leave his father and mother and be united to his wife, and the two will become one flesh.' 32This is a profound mystery—but I am talking about Christ and the church."

Interpreting Dreams Dictionary

Microphone - *Voice / Ability to Communicate*
    Positive - Authority, influence, preaching
    Negative - Control, need to be center of attention
    Matt 10:27

    Rev 21:3 "And I heard a loud voice from the throne saying, 'Now the dwelling of God is with men, and he will live with them. They will be his people, and God himself will be with them and be their God."

Microscope - *Examination*
    Positive - discernment, self-examination, soul searching
    Negative - judgement, lack of discernment, unaware
    1 Cor 11:28

    Gal 6:4 "But let each one examine his own work, and then he will have rejoicing in himself alone, and not in another." (NKJV)

Microwave - *Speed*
    Positive - Quick work, preparation, sudden miracle
    Negative - Impatience, prefers convenience to effort
    Rom 9:28

    Acts 16:26 "Suddenly there was such a violent earthquake that the foundations of the prison were shaken. At once all the prison doors flew open, and everybody's chains came loose."

Mirror - *Introspection / Examination*
   Positive - Searching of heart, discernment
   Negative - Vanity, looking back, personal past
   1 Cor 13:12

   Pro 27:19 "As water reflects a face, so a man's heart reflects the man."

Miscarriage - *Abort*
   Positive - Repentance
   Negative - Incomplete, failure, judgment without all the facts
   Hos 9:14, Jam 1:15, Hab 1:4

   Exo 23:26 "and none will miscarry or be barren in your land. I will give you a full life span."

Money - *Power / Ability*
   Positive - Provision, spiritual faith to gain the pleasures and purposes of God, wealth, natural talents, spiritual riches, authority
   Negative - Self-reliance, materialism, greed, holding back
   Gen 31:15, Luke 19:23, Rev 3:18

   1 Tim 6:10 "For the love of money is a root of all kinds of evil. Some people, eager for money, have wandered from the faith and pierced themselves with many griefs."

Interpreting Dreams Dictionary

Moon - *False Church*
> Positive - Rule, have authority, manifestation
> Negative - Manifestation, false worship, the occult, Islam
> *Eph 1:3, Isa 30:26, Deu 33:14*
>
> *Psa 89:37 "it will be established forever like the moon, the faithful witness in the sky." Selah"*

Morning - *New / Beginning*
> Positive - Mercy, communication with God, enlightenment, refreshment
> Negative - Contention, exhaustion, dread
> *Psa 5:3, Pro 27:14, 2 Pet 1:19*
>
> *Lam 3:22-23 " 22 Because of the LORD's great love we are not consumed, for his compassions never fail. 23 They are new every morning; great is your faithfulness."*

Mother – *Source / Impartation*
> Positive - Church, compassion, spiritual mother, nurturing, spiritual source
> Negative - abusive, neglect, harm, gossip
> *Isa 49:15, Isa 66:13*
>
> *Luke 8:21 "He replied, "My mother and brothers are those who hear God's word and put it into practice."*

Interpreting Dreams Dictionary

Mother-in-law - *Legalism*
    Positive - Support, reliance, security
    Negative - Meddler, trouble-maker, false teachers
    Psa 87:5-6, Hos 2:2, 5, Rom 16:13

    Ruth 3:1 "One day Naomi her mother-in-law said to her, "My daughter, should I not try to find a home [a] for you, where you will be well provided for?"

Motor – *Anointing*
    Positive - Power, power and acts of the Holy Spirit, momentum
    Negative - Self-motivation, self-reliance, flesh, powerless
    Acts 1:8, Eph 3:7

    Zec 4:6 "So he said to me, "This is the word of the LORD to Zerubbabel: 'Not by might nor by power, but by my Spirit,' says the LORD Almighty."

Motorcycle – *Individual*
    Positive - Personal ministry, independent spirit, fast progress
    Negative - Selfishness, rebellion, "lone-ranger", outside of authority
    2 Pet 2:10, 1 Sam 15:23

    Psa 104:3 "and lays the beams of his upper chambers on their waters. He makes the clouds his chariot and rides on the wings of the wind."

Mountain - *Exaltation / God's Glory*
    Positive - Place of meeting, the Kingdom of God, presence of God, faith
    Negative - Difficult challenge, obstacle, lack of faith
    Josh 14:12, Rev 6:14, Exo 19:20

    Mark 9:2 "After six days Jesus took Peter, James and John with him and led them up a high mountain, where they were all alone. There he was transfigured before them."

Mouth – *Words / Ability to Speak*
    Positive - Prophecy, speaking the word of God, edification, exhortation, teaching
    Negative - Gossip, speaking evil, cruel or abusive speech.
    Judg 7:6, Job 20:12. Psa 119:13, 2 Sam 22:9,

    Rev 1:16 "In his right hand he held seven stars, and out of his mouth came a sharp double-edged sword. His face was like the sun shining in all its brilliance."

Moving – *Change / New Beginning*
    Positive - God-ordained change, physical move, change of attitude, ministry change
    Negative - Refusal to change, self-willed, stuck
    Acts 7:2

    Eze 12:3 "'Therefore, son of man, pack your belongings for exile and in the daytime, as they watch, set out and go from where you are to another place. Perhaps they will understand, though they are a rebellious house."

Mushroom - *Quick*
    Positive - Sudden growth or increase, unexpected manifestation
    Negative - Fragile, poison, consumed or overtaken, something that appears of value but is not of great value at all, deception
    Jonah 4:10

    Isa 48:3 "I foretold the former things long ago, my mouth announced them and I made them known; then suddenly I acted, and they came to pass."

Music - *Worship / Stirring up of the Spirit*
    Positive - Worship of God, prophecy, deep desire, fully devoted
    Negative - Worship of idols, false worship
    Eze 33:32, Dan 3:5

    Eph 5:19 "Speak to one another with psalms, hymns and spiritual songs. Sing and make music in your heart to the Lord,"

-N-

Nails - *Words / Binding Together*
   Positive - Word of God, wisdom, vows, covenant, permanent, secure
   Negative - Broken vows, insecure, temporary
   1 Chr 22:3, Isa 41:7

   Ecc 12:11 "The words of the wise are like goads, their collected sayings like firmly embedded nails—given by one Shepherd."

Naked – *Exposed*
   Positive - Honest, truth, innocence
   Negative - Impure, ashamed, lust, exhibitionism, ignorance
   Gen 2:25, Rev 16:15, Rev 3:17

   Isa 58:7 "Is it not to share your food with the hungry and to provide the poor wanderer with shelter - when you see the naked, to clothe him, and not to turn away from your own flesh and blood?"

Nation - *Characteristic*
  Representation of a people group or tribe.
  Positive - Integrity, strength, action, provision etc.
  Negative - Immorality, corruption, poverty etc.
  1Kin 9:7, Gen 46:3

  1 Pet 2:9 "But you are a chosen people, a royal priesthood, a holy nation, a people belonging to God, that you may declare the praises of him who called you out of darkness into his wonderful light."

Neck – *Will / Influence*
  Positive - Authority, victory, godly influence on those in authority
  Negative - Stubborn, self-willed, evil influence, unbeliever
  Gen 27:40, Deu 28:48, Isa 10:27, Gen 33:4, Luke 15:20

  Exo 32:9 ""I have seen these people," the LORD said to Moses, "and they are a stiff-necked people.

Newspaper - *Announcement*
  Positive - To make known, prophecy, important or special event
  Negative - Gossip, exposure of sin in a public arena
  Luke 8:17, Isa 52:7

  Amos 4:5 "Burn leavened bread as a thank offering and brag about your freewill offerings - boast about them, you Israelites, for this is what you love to do," declares the Sovereign LORD."

Interpreting Dreams Dictionary

Night - *Darkness / Evil*
  Positive - Release from darkness or deception
  Negative - Ignorant, sin, power of evil, deception
  John 12:35, John 11:10

  1 Thes 5:7 "For those who sleep, sleep at night, and those who get drunk, get drunk at night."

North - *Spiritual / Positive*
  Positive - Equipped for spiritual warfare, heaven, inheritance
  Negative - Judgment, attack
  Pro 25:23, Jer 1:13-14, Deu 2:3

  Dan 11:15 "Then the king of the North will come and build up siege ramps and will capture a fortified city. The forces of the South will be powerless to resist; even their best troops will not have the strength to stand."

Nose - *Discernment*
  Positive - Discerning of spirits, beauty
  Negative - Meddling, strife, busybody
  Pro 30:33, 2 Kin 19:28, SS 7:4

  Psa 115:6 "they have ears, but cannot hear, noses, but they cannot smell;"

-O-

Ocean - *Humanity / World*
   Positive - Nations, people, generations, fast progress
   Negative - Unsettled, discontent, churning, false-hearted
   Psa 68:22, Jam 3:11-12, Rev 4:6

   Exo 14:22 "and the Israelites went through the sea on dry ground, with a wall of water on their right and on their left."

Oil - *Anointing*
   Positive - Anointing of the Holy Spirit, healing
   Negative - Deception, tendency to slip, unsure footing
   1Sam 16:13, Pro 5:3

   Jam 5:14 "Is any one of you sick? He should call the elders of the church to pray over him and anoint him with oil in the name of the Lord."

Interpreting Dreams Dictionary

Orphan - *Abandoned*
- *Positive* - Humble, dependent
- *Negative* - Oppressed, needy, weak, unhealthy dependence, misconception
- *Job 24:14, Ps 10:9, Isa 3:14*

Mal 3:5 "'So I will come near to you for judgment. I will be quick to testify against sorcerers, adulterers and perjurers, against those who defraud laborers of their wages, who oppress the widows and the fatherless, and deprive aliens of justice, but do not fear me," says the LORD Almighty."

Oven - *Judgement*
- *Positive* - Passion, meditation, preparation
- *Negative* - Trial, judgment, evil imaginings
- *Mal:4:1*

Hos 7:7 "All of them are hot as an oven; they devour their rulers. All their kings fall, and none of them calls on me."

Owl - *Spirit*
- *Positive* - Divine wisdom, ability to hunt in the dark
- *Negative* - Evil spirit, curse
- *Psa 102:6*

Isa 34:11 "The desert owl and screech owl will possess it; the great owl and the raven will nest there. God will stretch out over Edom the measuring line of chaos and the plumb line of desolation."

Ox - *Strength / Provision*
  Positive - Strength, ability, servant
  Negative - Burdened, slave
  Job 39:9, Isa 1:3

  Deu 33:17 "In majesty he is like a firstborn bull; his horns are the horns of a wild ox. With them he will gore the nations, even those at the ends of the earth. Such are the ten thousands of Ephraim; such are the thousands of Manasseh."

-P-

Painting - *Covering / Refreshing*
   Positive - Renovation, regeneration, protection
   Negative - Covering up, sin
   1 Pet 4:8, Titus 3:5

   Jer 22:14 "He says, 'I will build myself a great palace with spacious upper rooms.' So he makes large windows in it, panels it with cedar and decorates it in red."

Parachute - *Salvation / Redemption*
   Positive - Salvation, refuge, faith, God's promises
   Negative - Bail out, escape, abandon
   Matt 10:23

   Jam 5:20 "remember this: Whoever turns a sinner from the error of his way will save him from death and cover over a multitude of sins."

Parrot - *Mimic*
   Positive - Mimic, copy, repeat, act the same as
   Negative - Mocking, repetition of negative behaviors or words, without knowledge, obstinate
   2 Kin 2:23

   Heb 9:24 "For Christ did not enter a man-made sanctuary that was only a copy of the true one; he entered heaven itself, now to appear for us in God's presence."

Interpreting Dreams Dictionary

Path - *Your Life's Walk*
  Positive - Path of Life, the Way, Walk with God, gospel, salvation
  Negative - Misjudgment, error, self-willed
  Heb 3:10, Jer 6:16

  Neh 9:19 "'Because of your great compassion you did not abandon them in the desert. By day the pillar of cloud did not cease to guide them on their path, nor the pillar of fire by night to shine on the way they were to take."

Pen or Pencil - *Words / Truth*
  Positive - Communication, agreement, contract, vow, covenant, permanent
  Negative - Gossip, slander, exposure
  Jer 8:8, Job 13:26, Psa 45:1

  Pro 3:3 "Let love and faithfulness never leave you; bind them around your neck, write them on the tablet of your heart."

Perfume - *Influence / Presence of God*
  Positive - Appeal, pleasant, trusted council
  Negative - Seduction, lust, temptation, deception, false representation
  Pro 27:9, Pro 7:17-18

  SS 1:3 "Pleasing is the fragrance of your perfumes; your name is like perfume poured out. No wonder the maidens love you!"

Interpreting Dreams Dictionary

Picture - *Memory / Perception*
    Positive - Past-experience, ethic, imagination
    Negative - Past-experience, guilt, shame
    Heb 9:14, Num 33:52

    Matt 26:13 "I tell you the truth, wherever this gospel is preached throughout the world, what she has done will also be told, in memory of her."

Pig (swine) - *Unclean*
    Unclean spirits, backsliding, unbeliever
    Lev. 11:7, 2 Peter 2:22

    Matt 8:30-32 [30]"Some distance from them a large herd of pigs was feeding. [31]The demons begged Jesus, "If you drive us out, send us into the herd of pigs."[32]He said to them, "Go!" So they came out and went into the pigs, and the whole herd rushed down the steep bank into the lake and died in the water."

Playing - *Celebration*
    Positive - True worship, festivity, worship, time of joy, unrestrained
    Negative - Striving, competing, idolatry, out of order
    1 Cor 9:24, Col 3:5

    Zec 8:5 "The city streets will be filled with boys and girls playing there."

Interpreting Dreams Dictionary

Police - *Authority / God's Adjustment and Judgement*
　　Positive - Spiritual authority, divine protection, angels
　　Negative - Curse of the law, demons, control
　　Luke 12:11, Rom 13:1, 4

　　Neh 4:22 "At that time I also said to the people, "Have every man and his helper stay inside Jerusalem at night, so they can serve us as guards by night and workmen by day."

Postage Stamp - *Seal / Authority to Communicate*
　　Positive - Authority, authorization, powerful, anointed and released into ministry
　　Negative - Under authority of evil leader
　　John 6:27, Est 8:8

　　1 Kin 21:8 "So she wrote letters in Ahab's name, placed his seal on them, and sent them to the elders and nobles who lived in Naboth's city with him."

Pot / Pan - *Vessel / Preparation*
　　Positive - Tradition, entrusted servant, truth, preparation for ministry
　　Negative - False doctrine or teacher
　　Rom 2:20, Jer 1:13

　　Exo 25:29 "And make its plates and dishes of pure gold, as well as its pitchers and bowls for the pouring out of offerings."

Interpreting Dreams Dictionary

Preacher - *Messenger*
    Positive - God's representative, spokesperson, spiritual authority, one with authority in business
    Negative - Deception, false teacher
    Jer 3:15; 23:1, 2 Cor 11:13

    2 Pet 2:5 "if he did not spare the ancient world when he brought the flood on its ungodly people, but protected Noah, a preacher of righteousness, and seven others;"

Pregnancy - *New Life*
    Positive - New birth, waiting, preparation, in process, expectation
    Negative - Growing sin, desires of the flesh
    Isa 66:9, Psa 7:14

    Jam 1:15 "Then, after desire has conceived, it gives birth to sin; and sin, when it is full-grown, gives birth to death."

Purse / Wallet - *Treasure / Inner Secret*
    Positive - Valuable, precious, personal identity, provision, condition of heart
    Negative - Without value, spiritually bankrupt, financial despair, condition of heart
    Matt 6:21; 12:35, John 12:6

    Pro 15:6 "The house of the righteous contains great treasure, but the income of the wicked brings them trouble."

-Q-

Quail - *Provision*
> Positive - Divine provision, miracles, signs and wonders
> Negative - Abandoned, in need of provision, doubt
> *Exo 16:13, Num 11:31*
>
> *Psa 105:40 "They asked, and he brought them quail and satisfied them with the bread of heaven."*

Quarry - *Labor*
> Positive - Kingdom works, building the Kingdom, Kingdom laborer, provision, strength, foundation
> Negative - Works of the flesh, self-willed, legalism
> *1 Kin 5:17; 6:7*
>
> *2 Chr 2:2 "He conscripted seventy thousand men as carriers and eighty thousand as stonecutters in the hills and thirty-six hundred as foremen over them."*

Queen - *Influence*
(i.e. Esther and Pontius Pilate's Wife)
Positive - Authority, power, supply, ambassador
Negative - Power of evil, slavery, evil rule
Est 2:17, 2 Chr 9:9

Acts 8:27 "So he started out, and on his way he met an Ethiopian eunuch, an important official in charge of all the treasury of Candace, queen of the Ethiopians. This man had gone to Jerusalem to worship,"

-R-

Rabbit - *Increase / Prosperity*
Positive - Multiplication, rapid growth
Negative - Evil spirit, unclean, multiplication of sin or evil influence
Lev 11:6, Deu 14:7

Pro 20:21 "An inheritance quickly gained at the beginning will not be blessed at the end."

Raccoon - *Mischief*
Positive - Playful mischief, practical joker
Negative - Thievery, deception, deceit
Pro 4:16

Pro 10:23 "A fool finds pleasure in evil conduct, but a man of understanding delights in wisdom."

Radio - *Broadcast / Communication*
Positive - Public announcement, preaching, declaration, news, witnessing, continual flow of information
Negative - Unrelenting gossip, false news, unbeliever
Mat 24:14, Pro 9:13

Pro 25:25 "Like cold water to a weary soul is good news from a distant land."

Interpreting Dreams Dictionary

Raft - *Drifting / Survival*
   Positive - Saved, delivered, rescued
   Negative - Without control, no ambition, without direction.
   Luke 5:4, Psa 18:10, Mat 8:23

   Heb 2:1 "We must pay more careful attention, therefore, to what we have heard, so that we do not drift away."

Railroad Track - *Established Direction*
   Positive - Unchanging, steady path, the Gospel
   Negative - Habit, stubborn, caution, legalistic tradition, danger
   Mark 7:9,13, Col 2:8, 2 Thes 3:6

   2 Thes 2:15 "So then, brothers, stand firm and hold to the teachings we passed on to you, whether by word of mouth or by letter."

Rain - *Life / Blessings*
   Positive - Revival, Holy Spirit poured out, Word of God
   Negative - Depression, disappointment, trial, withheld blessings, presence of God lacking
   Jer 3:3, Zec 10:1, Isa 55:10-11

   Psa 68:8 "the earth shook, the heavens poured down rain, before God, the One of Sinai, before God, the God of Israel."

Interpreting Dreams Dictionary

Rainbow - *Covenant / Promise*
    Protection, good report, throne of God, end of discouragement or destruction
    Gen 9:13, Eze 1:28, Rev 4:3

    Gen 9:16 "Whenever the rainbow appears in the clouds, I will see it and remember the everlasting covenant between God and all living creatures of every kind on the earth."

Rat - *Unclean / Pest*
    Pest that lurks beneath, plague, devourer, wicked
    Lev 26:21, Psa 37:12

    Lev 11:29 " 'Of the animals that move about on the ground, these are unclean for you: the weasel, the rat, any kind of great lizard,"

Rearview Mirror - *Past*
    Positive - Moving on, leaving the past
    Negative - Looking back, bound to the past, legalism, regret, forgotten things, issues not dealt with
    2 Cor 3:6, Gen 19:26

    Phi 3:13-14 "13Brothers, I do not consider myself yet to have taken hold of it. But one thing I do: Forgetting what is behind and straining toward what is ahead, 14I press on toward the goal to win the prize for which God has called me heavenward in Christ Jesus."

Interpreting Dreams Dictionary

Reed - *Weak / Heart Condition*
　Positive - Bending, yielding, flexible
　Negative - Spiritually weak person, easily moved, affliction, fleshly weaknesses
　2 Kin 18:21, Mat 26:41

　Eze 29:6 "Then all who live in Egypt will know that I am the LORD." "You have been a staff of reed for the house of Israel."

Refrigerator - *Heart / Preservation*
　Positive - Motive of the heart, positive attitude, personal thoughts, provision
　Negative - Selfish motive, negative attitude, evil or fleshly thoughts
　Mat 12:35, Mark 7:21-22

　Deu 11:18 "Fix these words of mine in your hearts and minds; tie them as symbols on your hands and bind them on your foreheads."

Rifle - *See Gun*

Ring - *Promise / Public Contract*
　Positive - Authority, covenant, prosperity, prestige, acceptance, return home, forgiveness
　Negative - Self-glorification, broken promise, rebellion
　Est 8:8, Jam 2:2, Luke 15:21-22

　Gen 41:42 "Then Pharaoh took his signet ring from his finger and put it on Joseph's finger. He dressed him in robes of fine linen and put a gold chain around his neck."

River - *Flow of the Spirit*
  Positive - Spirit of God, righteousness, healing, river of life, salvation
  Negative - Sin, judgment, obstacle, trial
  Eze 47:5, Amos 5:24

  John 7:38-39 "Whoever believes in me, as the Scripture has said, streams of living water will flow from within him." ³⁹By this he meant the Spirit, whom those who believed in him were later to receive. Up to that time the Spirit had not been given, since Jesus had not yet been glorified."

Rocket - *Power / Speed*
  Positive - Powerful ministry, fast progress, sudden change or movement
  Negative - Speedy destruction, unexpected attack, war
  Psa 64:7, Pro 6:15; 29:1

  Acts 1:8 "But you will receive power when the Holy Spirit comes on you; and you will be my witnesses in Jerusalem, and in all Judea and Samaria, and to the ends of the earth."

Interpreting Dreams Dictionary

Rocking Chair - *Past / Complacency*
    Positive - Pleasant memories of the past, meditation, rest, retirement
    Negative - Painful memories of the past, exhaustion, depression, lack of motivation
    Jer 6:16

2 Tim 2:14 "Keep reminding them of these things. Warn them before God against quarreling about words; it is of no value, and only ruins those who listen."

Roller Coaster - *Out of Control*
    Positive - Excitement, fast movement, things appearing to move too fast but within a controlled space, protection
    Negative - Instability, unfaithfulness, trials, unreliable, things moving too fast
    Isa 40:4

Jam 1:6-8 "⁶But when he asks, he must believe and not doubt, because he who doubts is like a wave of the sea, blown and tossed by the wind. ⁷That man should not think he will receive anything from the Lord; ⁸he is a double-minded man, unstable in all he does."

Roller Skates or Blades - *Speedy*
　　Positive - Swift advancement or progress, skill
　　Negative - Swift decline, dangerous
　　Rom 9:28

　　Isa 5:19 "to those who say, "Let God hurry, let him hasten his work so we may see it. Let it approach, let the plan of the Holy One of Israel come, so we may know it."

Roof - *Covering / Protection*
　　Positive - Shelter, a place to get a better view or perspective
　　Negative - Deterioration of protection, unshielded, exposed
　　Acts 10:9, Matt 10:27

　　2 Sam 18:24 "While David was sitting between the inner and outer gates, the watchman went up to the roof of the gateway by the wall. As he looked out, he saw a man running alone."

Root - *Origin of Attitude*
　　Positive - Conviction, pure motive, stable, unmovable
　　Negative - Hidden sin, selfish motive, rebellion, low self-esteem, fear
　　Rom 11:16, Deu 29:18

　　Heb 12:15 "See to it that no one misses the grace of God and that no bitter root grows up to cause trouble and defile many."

Interpreting Dreams Dictionary

Rope / Cord - *Bond / Unity*
   Positive - Covenant, pledge, godly bond, salvation, rescue
   Negative - Bondage, hinderances, bond to sin, stronghold
   1 Kin 20:31, Jer 38:11, Pro 5:22

   Jos 2:15-18 "So she let them down by a rope through the window, for the house she lived in was part of the city wall. 16 Now she had said to them, "Go to the hills so the pursuers will not find you. Hide yourselves there three days until they return, and then go on your way."
   17 The men said to her, "This oath you made us swear will not be binding on us 18 unless, when we enter the land, you have tied this scarlet cord in the window through which you let us down, and unless you have brought your father and mother, your brothers and all your family into your house."

Rowing - *Steady Work*
   Positive - Intercessory prayer, spiritual labor, hard work
   Negative - Striving, unpleasant hard work
   Mark 6:48, Phi 2:30

   Isa 53:11 "After the suffering of his soul, he will see the light of life and be satisfied; by his knowledge my righteous servant will justify many, and he will bear their iniquities."

Interpreting Dreams Dictionary

Rug - *Covering / Wealth*
    Positive - Covenant, Holy Spirit, protection, of great value
    Negative - Cover up, hidden sin, deception
    Mark 4:22

    2 Cor 4:2 "Rather, we have renounced secret and shameful ways; we do not use deception, nor do we distort the word of God. On the contrary, by setting forth the truth plainly we commend ourselves to every man's conscience in the sight of God."

Running - *Striving / Vision*
    Positive - Faith, determination, pressing toward the goal
    Negative - Hasty decision, trial, difficult task
    1 Cor 9:24, Jer 12:15, Pro 1:6; 4:22

    Rev 9:9 "They had breastplates like breastplates of iron, and the sound of their wings was like the thundering of many horses and chariots rushing into battle."

-S-

Salt - *Preservative / Creates Thirst*
Positive - Covenant, cleanser, preserved, accepted, protected, provoking the unsaved to God so that they will desire the Lord
Negative - Rejected, unprotected, disobedient
Mark 9:50, Gen 19:26, Eze 47:11

Col 4:6 "Let your conversation be always full of grace, seasoned with salt, so that you may know how to answer everyone."

Sand - *People / Flesh*
Positive - Innocence of a child, carefree, playful, multitude, plentiful
Negative - Weak, unsure foundation, childish, unclean
Mat 7:26-27, Gen 13:16; 22:17

Gen 32:12 "But you have said, 'I will surely make you prosper and will make your descendants like the sand of the sea, which cannot be counted.'"

School – *Teaching / Preparation*
    Church, work environment, teaching ministry, place of training and preparation for ministry, career or life's work
    Judge training level to grade of school, i.e. kindergarten vs. college
    Acts 19:9, Luke 8:35

    Isa 1:17 "Learn to do right! Seek justice, encourage the oppressed. Defend the cause of the fatherless, plead the case of the widow."

Scorpion - *Sin Nature*
    Positive - Overcoming the sin nature
    Negative - Great danger not immediately visible, temptation, deception, poisonous, stinging pain
    Luke 10:19; 11:12

    Rev 9:5 "They were not given power to kill them, but only to torture them for five months. And the agony they suffered was like that of the sting of a scorpion when it strikes a man."

Sea - *See Ocean*

Seat Belt - *Security / Promise of God*
    Positive - Safety assurance, protection
    Negative - Control, stifled, bound
    Psa 118:27

    Job 24:23 "He may let them rest in a feeling of security, but his eyes are on their ways."

Seed - *Word / Finance*
> Positive - Word of God, faith, Christ, fulfillment, promise, replenished finance
> Negative - Word of man, sin conceived, works of the flesh
> *Luke 8:11, Gen 1:11-12, Luke 6:45*

Matt 13:27-30 " [27]"The owner's servants came to him and said, 'Sir, didn't you sow good seed in your field? Where then did the weeds come from?[28]" 'An enemy did this,' he replied. "The servants asked him, 'Do you want us to go and pull them up?'[29]" 'No,' he answered, 'because while you are pulling the weeds, you may root up the wheat with them. [30]Let both grow together until the harvest. At that time I will tell the harvesters: First collect the weeds and tie them in bundles to be burned; then gather the wheat and bring it into my barn.' "

Sex - *Spiritual Reproduction*
> Positive - Covenant, agreement, unity, private, reproducing
> Negative - Abusive authority, lust, selfishness, shame
> *1 Cor 6:15-16, Exo 22:16, Jer 7:9-10*

Gen 2:23-24 "[23] The man said, "This is now bone of my bones and flesh of my flesh; she shall be called 'woman, for she was taken out of man."[24] For this reason a man will leave his father and mother and be united to his wife, and they will become one flesh."

Interpreting Dreams Dictionary

Sheep / Lamb - *Innocent / Offering*
Positive - Jesus, true believers, blameless, pure, sacrifice
Negative - Unwilling sacrifice, naive, unaware, lost
Psa 100:3, Isa 53:7, Mat 18:13

John 10:4 "When he has brought out all his own, he goes on ahead of them, and his sheep follow him because they know his voice."

Shoes - *Word*
Positive - Gospel, preparation, protection from contact with the world, covenant
Negative - Lusts of the flesh, evil intent, sinful covenant, contact with the carnality of the world
Gal 5:16, Ruth 4:7, John 13:10

Eph 6:15 "and with your feet fitted with the readiness that comes from the gospel of peace."

Shoulder - *Support*
    Positive - Government, authority, responsibility, strength, set-aside, holy
    Negative - Stubborn, discouraged, seduction, temptation
    Isa 9:6, Deu 18:3, Zec 7:11

    Isa 46:7 "They lift it to their shoulders and carry it; they set it up in its place, and there it stands. From that spot it cannot move. Though one cries out to it, it does not answer; it cannot save him from his troubles."

Shovel - *Tongue*
    Positive - Confession, prayer, inquire
    Negative - Gossip, slander, words that dig
    Pro 16:27; 26:27, Exo 27:13, Isa 30:24

    Jas 1:26 "If anyone considers himself religious and yet does not keep a tight rein on his tongue, he deceives himself and his religion is worthless."

Shower - *See Bath*

Interpreting Dreams Dictionary

Sign - *Direction / Confirmation*
    Positive - Decision, change, promise fulfilled, confirmation, covenant
    Negative - Correction, offense

    Note: important to pay attention to what type of sign it is, for example "Stop", "Yield" or an advertisement etc.
    Hos 12:10, Gen 9:12

    Rev 15:1 "I saw in heaven another great and marvelous sign: seven angels with the seven last plagues—last, because with them God's wrath is completed."

Silver - *Knowledge / Blessings*
    Positive - Redemption, knowledge of God, purification, revelation
    Negative - Idolatry, spiritual adultery, worldly knowledge, betrayal
    Matt 27:6, 1 Pet 1:17-18

    Psa 12:6 "And the words of the LORD are flawless, like silver refined in a furnace of clay, purified seven times."

Sink - *Prayer / Cleansing*
    Positive - Repentance, petition, intercession, rehashing the word of God
    Negative - Self-justification, rebellion, sin
    Matt 27:24, Isa 1:16

    Jer 4:14 "O Jerusalem, wash the evil from your heart and be saved. How long will you harbor wicked thoughts?"

Sister - *Individual*
> Positive - Spiritual sister, a person with like characteristics or traits, the church, a gifting or anointing that you don't often function in
> Negative - Sister of the flesh, evil alliance
> *Matt 12:50*
>
> *Gen 20:5 "Did he not say to me, 'She is my sister,' and didn't she also say, 'He is my brother'? I have done this with a clear conscience and clean hands."*

Skirt - *Truth / Covering*
> Positive - Grace, beauty
> Negative - Exposed, shame, unethical behavior
> *Jer 2:34; 13:26, Gen 3:7*
>
> *Jer 13:22 "And if you ask yourself, "Why has this happened to me?" - it is because of your many sins that your skirts have been torn off and your body mistreated."*

Sleep - *Rest / Death*
> Positive - Unconscious, rejuvenation, safety, blessing
> Negative - Unaware, ignorant, laziness
> *Psa 4:8, Pro 6:9*
>
> *Rom 13:11 "And do this, understanding the present time. The hour has come for you to wake up from your slumber, because our salvation is nearer now than when we first believed."*

Smoke - *Evidence / Discernment*
    Positive - Glory of God, prayer, worship, manifestation of the presence of God
    Negative - Boasting, clouded, judgement, hidden
    Matt 12:20, Gen 19:28, Acts 10:4

    Rev 8:4 "The smoke of the incense, together with the prayers of the saints, went up before God from the angel's hand."

Snake - *Satan*
    Positive - Victory of Christ, overcoming the curse, spiritual warfare
    Negative - Deception, curse, sin, slander, critical spirit, witchcraft, danger, poison
    Gen 3:1, 14, Psa 140:3

    Rev 20:2 "He seized the dragon, that ancient serpent, who is the devil, or Satan, and bound him for a thousand years."

Interpreting Dreams Dictionary

Snow - *Word / Blessings*
    Positive - Purity, grace, restoration, revelation, slow gentle method of refreshing,
    Negative - Unfulfilled, hindered, pent-in, opposition, diseased
    2 Kin 5:27, Mat 28:3

    Isa 55:10-11 "^{10} *As the rain and the snow come down from heaven, and do not return to it without watering the earth and making it bud and flourish, so that it yields seed for the sower and bread for the eater,* ^{11} *so is my word that goes out from my mouth: It will not return to me empty, but will accomplish what I desire and achieve the purpose for which I sent it."*

Soap - *Cleansing / Purification*
    Positive - Repentance, conviction of the Holy Spirit, forgiveness, cleansing of the heart
    Negative - Condemnation, guilt, shame
    Jer 2:22, Mal 3:2

    Job 9:30 "Even if I washed myself with soap and my hands with washing soda,"

Soldier - *Angel / Messenger / Answer*
  Positive - Authority, angelic presence, protection, answer to prayer
  Negative - Persecution, demonic presence, evil authority, warfare
  2 Tim 2:3-4, Psa 55:21

  Rev 12:7, 10 "⁷And there was war in heaven. Michael and his angels fought against the dragon, and the dragon and his angels fought back. ¹⁰Then I heard a loud voice in heaven say: "Now have come the salvation and the power and the kingdom of our God, and the authority of his Christ. For the accuser of our brothers, who accuses them before our God day and night, has been hurled down."

Son - *Ministry / Business*
  Positive - Spiritual son, ministry that you started or reproduced, spiritual or business production or reproduction
  Negative - Rebellious ministry, out of order, lustful, self-willed
  Isa 9:6, Eze 16:44, Luke 15:13, 1 Chr 28:20

  Pro 4:3-4 "³ When I was a boy in my father's house, still tender, and an only child of my mother, ⁴ he taught me and said, "Lay hold of my words with all your heart; keep my commands and you will live."

Interpreting Dreams Dictionary

South - *Incorrect*
   Positive - Return home, warming
   Negative - Out of order, temptation, trial, deception, attack, deception
   Gen 13:3, Josh 10:40, Job 37:9

   Luke 12:55 "And when the south wind blows, you say, 'It's going to be hot,' and it is."

Stairs - *Progress / Elevation*
   Positive - Promotion, steps or procedures, safety, steady progress, to grow and mature step-by-step, continual
   Negative - Backslide, demotion, failure, dangerous, steady decline
   Exo 20:26, Acts 21:40

   Neh 9:4 "Standing on the stairs were the Levites—Jeshua, Bani, Kadmiel, Shebaniah, Bunni, Sherebiah, Bani and Kenani—who called with loud voices to the LORD their God."

Stone - *Witness / Foundation*
   Positive - Testimony, precept, Word of God, cornerstone, Christ
   Negative - Persecution, accusation, witchcraft
   Lev 20:27, 1 Pet 2:5

   Jos 24:27 "See!" he said to all the people. "This stone will be a witness against us. It has heard all the words the LORD has said to us. It will be a witness against you if you are untrue to your God."

Storm - *Disturbance / Challenge of Life*
   Positive - Change, power of God, revival, inevitable
   Negative - Trial, calamity, sudden destruction, inevitable difficulty
   Isa 25:4, Psa 107:29

   Nah 1:3 "The LORD is slow to anger and great in power; the LORD will not leave the guilty unpunished. His way is in the whirlwind and the storm, and clouds are the dust of his feet."

Suicide - *Self-Destruction / Failure*
   Positive - Radical change, renewal of the mind
   Negative - Grief, remorse, self-hatred, guilt
   (We can commit emotional or spiritual suicide by making unwise decisions knowingly out of a wound or hurt from the past.)
   Ecc 7:16, 2 Cor 5:17

   Matt 27:4-5 "⁴"I have sinned," he said, "for I have betrayed innocent blood." "What is that to us?" they replied. "That's your responsibility." ⁵So Judas threw the money into the temple and left. Then he went away and hanged himself."

Interpreting Dreams Dictionary

Suitcase - *Private / Preparation*
    Positive - Travel, move, transition, intimate or personal issues, redemption
    Negative - Hidden things of the heart, separation, old habits (i.e. baggage)
    Eze 12:3, Gal 6:5

    Job 14:17 "My offenses will be sealed up in a bag; you will cover over my sin."

Summer - *Harvest / Time of Blessing*
    Positive - Covenant, reaping, opportunity
    Negative - Trial, affliction, torment
    Psa 32:4, Pro 10:5

    Jer 40:12 "they all came back to the land of Judah, to Gedaliah at Mizpah, from all the countries where they had been scattered. And they harvested an abundance of wine and summer fruit."

Sun - *Glory / Nation of Israel / Church of God*
    Positive - Light, truth, God, virtue
    Negative - Affliction, persecution, god of this world (Satan), law
    Mal 4:2, Mark 4:6,17

    Psa 19:4-7 "⁴ Their voice goes out into all the earth, their words to the ends of the world. In the heavens he has pitched a tent for the sun, ⁵ which is like a bridegroom coming forth from his pavilion, like a champion rejoicing to run his course. ⁶ It rises at one end of the heavens and makes its circuit to the other; nothing is hidden from its heat. ⁷ The law of the LORD is perfect, reviving the soul. The statutes of the LORD are trustworthy, making wise the simple."

Swimming - *Walking in the Spirit*
> Positive - Worship, functioning in the gifts of the Spirit, flowing, service
> Negative - Self-glorification, ego, competition, obstacle
> *Eze 47:5*
>
> *Isa 41:18 "I will make rivers flow on barren heights, and springs within the valleys. I will turn the desert into pools of water, and the parched ground into springs."*

Sword - *Word*
> Positive - Word of God, equipped, prepared
> Negative - Critical or damaging words, difficulty, strife, war, persecution
> *Eph 6:17, Pro 12:18*
>
> *Rev 6:4 "Then another horse came out, a fiery red one. Its rider was given power to take peace from the earth and to make men slay each other. To him was given a large sword."*

-T-

Table - *Communion / Celebration*
   Positive - Agreement, covenant, provision, communication, structure of God's authority
   Negative - Broken agreement, deceit, hidden motives, lack of provision
   1 Cor 10:20-21, Dan 11:27, Psa 78:19

   Psa 23:5 "You prepare a table before me in the presence of my enemies. You anoint my head with oil; my cup overflows."

Tail - *Last / End / Follows*
   Positive - The end of a season, change, servant's heart
   Negative - Poisonous, deadly, last in line, waiting, overlooked, false prophet
   Isa 9:15, Rev 12:4, Deu 28:44

   Deu 28:13 "The LORD will make you the head, not the tail. If you pay attention to the commands of the LORD your God that I give you this day and carefully follow them, you will always be at the top, never at the bottom.

Tar - *Repair / Seal*
    Positive - Cover, patch, healing, restoration
    Negative - Bitterness, spirit of offense, grudge, desolation
    Isa 34:8-9

    Exo 2:3 "But when she could hide him no longer, she got a papyrus basket for him and coated it with tar and pitch. Then she placed the child in it and put it among the reeds along the bank of the Nile."

Tasting - *Experience / Prove or Try*
    Positive - Discernment, trust, vision, take a chance
    Negative - Trial, judgement, mutilation, destruction
    Psa 34:8, Job 6:30

    Job 12:11 "Does not the ear test words as the tongue tastes food?"

Tea - *Refreshment*
    Positive - Grace, refreshing in His presence, waiting on the Lord, revival, salvation
    Negative - Separated from grace, parched, dry season
    Pro 25:25, Isa 28:12

    Acts 3:19 "Repent, then, and turn to God, so that your sins may be wiped out, that times of refreshing may come from the Lord,"

Teacher - *Leadership / Spiritual Authority*
    Positive - Revelation, direction, Jesus, Holy Spirit, authority
    Negative - Works of the flesh, evil leader, false prophet
    Mat 8:19, Joel 2:23

    Mat 23:10 "Nor are you to be called 'teacher,' for you have one Teacher, the Christ."

Tears - *Grief*
    Positive - Repentance, healing, prayer, intercession
    Negative - Sorrow, anguish, judgement
    Job 16:20, Psa 126:5

    Jer 9:1 "Oh, that my head were a spring of water and my eyes a fountain of tears! I would weep day and night for the slain of my people."

Teeth - *Wisdom*
    Positive - Experience, wise council, meditation, dependency (losing teeth seems negative but is actually positive because we lose our own wisdom and become dependent on God's)
    Negative - Destruction, danger, without wisdom, inexperienced, immature
    Psa 3:7, Rev 9:8

    Pro 30:14 "those whose teeth are swords and whose jaws are set with knives to devour the poor from the earth, the needy from among mankind."

Telephone - *Tool of Communication*
   Positive - Message from God, prayer, intercession, Godly counsel, to reach out
   Negative - Gossip, ungodly speech, false witness
   Acts 2:21, Rom 10:12, Isa 59:1-2

   Num 12:8 "With him I speak face to face, clearly and not in riddles; he sees the form of the LORD. Why then were you not afraid to speak against my servant Moses?"

Telescope - *Insight*
   Positive - Prophetic vision of the future, vision, prophetic sight
   Negative - Making a small problem bigger
   Rev 4:1 "After this I looked, and there before me was a door standing open in heaven. And the voice I had first heard speaking to me like a trumpet said, "Come up here, and I will show you what must take place after this."

Television - *Vision*
   Positive - Prophetic message, preaching, good news
   Negative - Evil influence, wickedness, bad news
   Num 24:16, Dan 2:19

   Rom 1:32 "Although they know God's righteous decree that those who do such things deserve death, they not only continue to do these very things but also approve of those who practice them."

Temple - *Sanctuary*
> Positive - God's habitation or dwelling, place of prayer, Jesus, inner or personal sanctuary, worship, devotion, service, physical body
> Negative - Legalism, physical body
> *Lev 21:23, Jer 51:51*
>
> *Eph 2:19-22 "[19]Consequently, you are no longer foreigners and aliens, but fellow citizens with God's people and members of God's household, [20]built on the foundation of the apostles and prophets, with Christ Jesus himself as the chief cornerstone. [21]In him the whole building is joined together and rises to become a holy temple in the Lord. [22]And in him you too are being built together to become a dwelling in which God lives by his Spirit."*

Termite - Subtle *Destruction*
> Positive - Destruction of evil, tearing down strongholds
> Negative - Unseen destruction, deception, hidden sin
> *Psa 11:3*
>
> *Hag 1:6 "You have planted much, but have harvested little. You eat, but never have enough. You drink, but never have your fill. You put on clothes, but are not warm. You earn wages, only to put them in a purse with holes in it."*

Thief - *Enemy*
>Positive - Taking back that which had been stolen, spiritual warfare
>Negative - Deception, spiritual death, Satan, destruction, flesh, unexpected loss
>*John 10:10, Pro 29:24*
>
>*1 The 5:2-4 "²for you know very well that the day of the Lord will come like a thief in the night. ³While people are saying, "Peace and safety," destruction will come on them suddenly, as labor pains on a pregnant woman, and they will not escape. ⁴But you, brothers, are not in darkness so that this day should surprise you like a thief."*

Thigh - *Flesh / Truth*
>Positive - Strength, support, covenant, promise, discovering that which is hidden or covered
>Negative - Flesh, lust, seduction, manipulation, deception
>*Rev 19:16, Num 18:18*
>
>*Gen 24:2 "He said to the chief servant in his household, the one in charge of all that he had, "Put your hand under my thigh."*

Interpreting Dreams Dictionary

Thorns - *Hinderance / Thoughts*
　Positive - Protective barrier, redeeming the thoughts of man
　Negative - Persecution, gossip, worry, curse, defense, irritant, unredeemed thoughts
　Heb 6:8, Hos 2:6, Gen 3:18

　Mark 4:7 "Other seed fell among thorns, which grew up and choked the plants, so that they did not bear grain."

Throne - *Rule / Government*
　Positive - Authority, inner court, God, mercy seat, Kingship of the Lord
　Negative - Rulers of darkness, demonic activity, rule of the flesh
　1 Tim 2:5, Matt 17:19

　Rev 21:5 "He who was seated on the throne said, "I am making everything new!" Then he said, "Write this down, for these words are trustworthy and true."

Thunder - *Voice*
　Positive - Voice of God, blessing, positive change
　Negative - Storm, judgement, without understanding
　Psa 77:18, 1 Sam 7:10

　Rev 6:1 "I watched as the Lamb opened the first of the seven seals. Then I heard one of the four living creatures say in a voice like thunder, "Come!"

Tiger - *Danger*
> Positive - Powerful minister, spiritual warrior
> Negative - Dangerous person, evil intent, attack, not submissive
> 1 John 3:8, Zec 7:11
>
> *1 Sam 13:6 "When the men of Israel saw that their situation was critical and that their army was hard pressed, they hid in caves and thickets, among the rocks, and in pits and cisterns."*

Tin - *Waste / False*
> Positive - Purification, supporting role, covering
> Negative - Cheap, imitation, ineffective covering, trial
> Num 31:22
>
> *Eze 22:18-20 ""Son of man, the house of Israel has become dross to me; all of them are the copper, tin, iron and lead left inside a furnace. They are but the dross of silver. ¹⁹ Therefore this is what the Sovereign LORD says: 'Because you have all become dross, I will gather you into Jerusalem. ²⁰ As men gather silver, copper, iron, lead and tin into a furnace to melt it with a fiery blast, so will I gather you in my anger and my wrath and put you inside the city and melt you."*

Interpreting Dreams Dictionary

Tractor (Farm) - *Slow but Powerful Work*
    Positive - Powerful ministry or business, deep teaching, spiritual farmer, seed sower, slow but effective teaching, ministry or business, equipped for a specific ministry or task, specific tool
    Negative - Spiritual attack, digging words, deep injury or woundedness
    Acts 1:8

Acts 4:33 "With great power the apostles continued to testify to the resurrection of the Lord Jesus, and much grace was upon them all."

Tractor Trailer (Semi-Truck) - *Extension of Ministry*
    Positive - Powerful, large work, extensions of the Church
    Negative - Large burden, heavy weight, restrained movement
    2 Sam 6:3, Acts 5:4

Eph 1:19-23 "19 and his incomparably great power for us who believe. That power is like the working of his mighty strength, 20 which he exerted in Christ when he raised him from the dead and seated him at his right hand in the heavenly realms, 21 far above all rule and authority, power and dominion, and every title that can be given, not only in the present age but also in the one to come. 22 And God placed all things under his feet and appointed him to be head over everything for the church, 23 which is his body, the fullness of him who fills everything in every way."

Trailer - *Temporary / Extension*
  Positive - Flexible, mobile ministry, family ministry
  Negative - Transitory, indefinite circumstances
  Jam 4:14 "Why, you do not even know what will happen tomorrow. What is your life? You are a mist that appears for a little while and then vanishes."

Train - *Ministry Having Many Facets or Departments*
  Positive - Steady, unceasing work, spiritual connections, great move of the Holy Spirit
  Negative - Confined movement, driven by the flesh, works motivated
  1 The 2:18, Acts 2:42, 1 Kin 12:18

  Psa 77:2 "When I was in distress, I sought the Lord; at night I stretched out untiring hands and my soul refused to be comforted."

Tree - *Nations / Leaders*
  Positive - Covering, leadership, sanctuary, shelter
  Negative - False worship, self-glorification, evil influence, idolatry
  Psa 52:8; 37:35, 2 Kin 17:10

  Eze 17:24 "All the trees of the field will know that I the LORD bring down the tall tree and make the low tree grow tall. I dry up the green tree and make the dry tree flourish. " 'I the LORD have spoken, and I will do it.' "

Trophy - *Victory / Reward*
   Positive - Tangible victory, award, promotion, validation of gift or call, overcoming
   Negative - Competition, pride, self-seeking, self-promotion
   1 Kin 20:11

   1 Sam 17:57 "As soon as David returned from killing the Philistine, Abner took him and brought him before Saul, with David still holding the Philistine's head."

Trumpet - *Voice / Announcement*
   Positive - Prophecy, worship, rapture, declaration, blessing, call to gather, announcement of preparation
   Negative - Prophetic warning, call to war, danger
   Isa 58:1, 1 Cor 15:52

   Joel 2:15 "Blow the trumpet in Zion, declare a holy fast, call a sacred assembly."

Tunnel - *Passage*
    Positive - A way made where there was no way, transition, a way of escape, hope, refreshment, revival
    Negative - Darkness, troubling event, fear, trapped
    1 Cor 10:13

    2 Chr 32:30 "This same Hezekiah also stopped the water outlet of Upper Gihon, and brought the water by tunnel to the west side of the City of David. Hezekiah prospered in all his works."

- U -

Umbrella - *Covering / Shelter*
   Positive - Protection, security
   Negative - Separating oneself from the Holy Spirit, detached, depression
   Psa 91:1, Isa 4:5

   Job 31:19 "if I have seen anyone perishing for lack of clothing, or a needy man without a garment,"

Upstairs - *Spiritual*
   Positive - Godly thought, meditation, prayer, worship
   Negative - Self-exaltation, dominance, control
   1 Kin 12:31, Pro 18:19

   Acts 1:13-14 " ¹³When they arrived, they went upstairs to the room where they were staying. Those present were Peter, John, James and Andrew; Philip and Thomas, Bartholomew and Matthew; James son of Alphaeus and Simon the Zealot, and Judas son of James. ¹⁴They all joined together constantly in prayer, along with the women and Mary the mother of Jesus, and with his brothers."

Urine - *Cleansing / Purification*
    Positive - Repentance, relief of pressure, healing, restoration, repetitive process
    Negative - Temptation, strong urge, lust, contention, offense
    Pro 17:14, 1 Sam 25:22

Jer 25:5 "They said, 'Turn now, each of you, from your evil ways and your evil practices, and you can stay in the land the LORD gave to you and your fathers for ever and ever."

- V -

Valley - *Trial / Place of Escape*
  Positive - Faith, trust, rest, provision, victory, persistence
  Negative - Difficulty, season of trial, hopelessness, depression
  Job 39:21, Isa 63:14

  Psa 23:4 "Even though I walk through the valley of the shadow of death, I will fear no evil, for you are with me; your rod and your staff, they comfort me.

Van - *Family / Spiritual Children*
  Positive - Spiritual family, family ministry, fellowship, growing business
  Negative - Limitation in ministry, confinement, controlled by another
  1Kin 12:18, Acts 8:28-38

  Eph 3:14-19 "14For this reason I kneel before the Father, 15from whom his whole family in heaven and on earth derives its name. 16I pray that out of his glorious riches he may strengthen you with power through his Spirit in your inner being, 17so that Christ may dwell in your hearts through faith. And I pray that you, being rooted and established in love, 18may have power, together with all the saints, to grasp how wide and long and high and deep is the love of Christ, 19and to know this love that surpasses knowledge—that you may be filled to the measure of all the fullness of God."

Interpreting Dreams Dictionary

Vapor / Mist - *Presence*
    Positive - Manifestation of the presence of God, Holy Spirit, life
    Negative - Fleeting, temporary, occult, demonic manifestation, vain promise
    Jam 4:14, Isa 19:1

    Acts 2:19 "I will show wonders in heaven above And signs in the earth beneath: Blood and fire and vapor of smoke. (NKJV)

Veil - *Concealment / Purity*
    Positive - Righteousness, anointing, authority, five-fold ministry, protection, something of utmost importance, belonging to someone or something else
    Negative - Deception, deceit, blocked understanding, law, flesh
    2 Cor 3:16, Luke 24:45

    Mark 15:37-38 "37With a loud cry, Jesus breathed his last. 38The curtain of the temple was torn in two from top to bottom."

Vine - *Source / Jesus*
  Positive - Christ, family, Church, city or nation
  Negative - Entanglement, snare, flesh
  Psa 80:8, Eze 19:10

  John 15:1-5 " ¹"I am the true vine, and my Father is the gardener. ²He cuts off every branch in me that bears no fruit, while every branch that does bear fruit he prunes so that it will be even more fruitful. ³You are already clean because of the word I have spoken to you. ⁴Remain in me, and I will remain in you. No branch can bear fruit by itself; it must remain in the vine. Neither can you bear fruit unless you remain in me. ⁵"I am the vine; you are the branches. If a man remains in me and I in him, he will bear much fruit; apart from me you can do nothing."

Vinegar - *Bitterness*
  Positive - Cleansing, healing, benefit
  Negative - Irritant, sourness, bitterness, deterioration
  Num 6:3, Ruth 2:14

  Pro 25:20 "Like one who takes away a garment on a cold day, or like vinegar poured on soda, is one who sings songs to a heavy heart."

Voice - *Direction*
  Positive - Covenant, promise, communion, obedience, prophetic word
  Negative - Wrath, judgement, disobedience
  John 10:4, Heb 12:26

  Rev 1:15 "His feet were like bronze glowing in a furnace, and his voice was like the sound of rushing waters."

Interpreting Dreams Dictionary

Volcano - *Eruption / Warning*
    Positive - Explosive change, sign, fast growth, remnant or reminder of what we have been through
    Negative - Judgement, emotionally volatile, extreme pressure, dangerous
    Deu 32:22, Rev 20:9

    Psa 11:6 "On the wicked he will rain fiery coals and burning sulfur; a scorching wind will be their lot."

Vulture - *Scavenger*
    Positive - Patience, vision, opportunity
    Negative - Unclean, devourer, lies in wait, consumption
    Lev 11:13

    Jer 12:9 "Has not my inheritance become to me like a speckled bird of prey that other birds of prey surround and attack? Go and gather all the wild beasts; bring them to devour."

- W -

Walking - *Progress / Confirmation of Moving Forward*
   Positive - Living in the Spirit, way of life, conduct
   Negative - Living in sin, way of life, conduct
   Gal 5:25, Eph 4:17

   Gal 5:16-18 " ¹⁶So I say, live by the Spirit, and you will not gratify the desires of the sinful nature. ¹⁷For the sinful nature desires what is contrary to the Spirit, and the Spirit what is contrary to the sinful nature. They are in conflict with each other, so that you do not do what you want. ¹⁸But if you are led by the Spirit, you are not under law."

Wall - *Barrier / Obstacle*
   Positive - Defense, leaders, support, Kingdom of God, protection
   Negative - Hinderance, obstacle, unbelief, pride
   2 Sam 22:30, Neh 6:6-15

   Pro 18:11 "The wealth of the rich is their fortified city; they imagine it an unscalable wall."

Warrior - *See Soldier*

Interpreting Dreams Dictionary

Watch - *Alert / Prayerful*
>Positive - On guard, vigilant, prophetic, alert to strategies of the enemy, watchful intercession, vision to see
>Negative - Warning, attack, plan of the enemy
>*1 Pet 5:8, 1 Cor 16:13, 2 Kin 11:6*
>
>*Rev 3:3 "Remember therefore how you have received and heard; hold fast and repent. Therefore if you will not watch, I will come upon you as a thief, and you will not know what hour I will come upon you." (NKJV)*

Water - *Spirit / Life*
>Positive - Purification, cleansing, renewal, flow of the Holy Spirit, power, wisdom
>Negative - Instability, iniquity, worry, sorrow
>*Eph 5:26, Gen 49:4, Pro 18:4, John 7:38*
>
>*John 4:14 "but whoever drinks the water I give him will never thirst. Indeed, the water I give him will become in him a spring of water welling up to eternal life."*

Watermelon - *Fruit*
>Positive - Refreshing, sweet spirit, peace, fruit of the spirit, life
>Negative - Sinful pleasures, fruit of the flesh
>*Gal 5:16-23, Pro 1:31*
>
>*Isa 4:2 "In that day the Branch of the LORD will be beautiful and glorious, and the fruit of the land will be the pride and glory of the survivors in Israel."*

Weasel - *Informant / Persistence*
    Positive - Carrier of information, message
    Negative - Betrayer, traitor, gossip
    Mark 14:10, Isa 16:3

    Gal 2:4 "This matter arose because some false brothers had infiltrated our ranks to spy on the freedom we have in Christ Jesus and to make us slaves."

Weeds - *Invader / Unkept*
    Positive - Removal of sin, flesh or iniquity
    Negative - Laziness, sin, impostor, neglect, works of the flesh, destructive
    Gen 2:15, Jon 2:5

    Pro 24:30-31 "30 I went past the field of the sluggard, past the vineyard of the man who lacks judgment; 31 thorns had come up everywhere, the ground was covered with weeds, and the stone wall was in ruins."

West - *End*
    Positive - Grace, conforming, revival, death
    Negative - Death, end of a season
    Psa 103:12, Luke 12:54

    Exo 10:19 "And the LORD changed the wind to a very strong west wind, which caught up the locusts and carried them into the Red Sea. Not a locust was left anywhere in Egypt."

Wife - *Church /Covenant / Business*
   Positive - Church, Holy Spirit, faithfulness, productive, submission, in agreement with, something we are responsible for
   Negative - Unfaithfulness, harlotry, control, manipulation, gossip
   Gal 4:24, Eze 16:8-14

   Eph 5:25-32 "25Husbands, love your wives, just as Christ loved the church and gave himself up for her 26to make her holy, cleansing her by the washing with water through the word, 27and to present her to himself as a radiant church, without stain or wrinkle or any other blemish, but holy and blameless. 28In this same way, husbands ought to love their wives as their own bodies. He who loves his wife loves himself. 29After all, no one ever hated his own body, but he feeds and cares for it, just as Christ does the church - 30for we are members of his body. 31"For this reason a man will leave his father and mother and be united to his wife, and the two will become one flesh." 32This is a profound mystery - but I am talking about Christ and the church."

Wind - *Spirit / Evidence*
   Positive - Life, Holy Spirit, power of God, refreshment, doctrine
   Negative - Storm, anxiety, demonic activity, opposition, correction, legalistic doctrine
   Eph 4:14, John 3:8, Pro 25:14

   John 20:22 "And with that he breathed on them and said, "Receive the Holy Spirit."

Window - *Revelation / Opening of a Promise*
   Positive - Truth, heavenly favor, prophecy, understanding, hope, redemption, a way to let light in
   Negative - Sin revealed, exposed, unguarded opening, contempt
   Jos 2:18-20, Gen 6:16

   1 Chr 15:29 "As the ark of the covenant of the LORD was entering the City of David, Michal daughter of Saul watched from a window. And when she saw King David dancing and celebrating, she despised him in her heart.

Wine - *Spirit*
   Positive - Revelation, truth, fellowship, communion, wisdom, Holy Spirit
   Negative - Intoxicant, strong emotion, witchcraft, delusion
   Eph 5:18, John 2:3, Psa 75:8

   Luke 5:37-38 "And no one pours new wine into old wineskins. If he does, the new wine will burst the skins, the wine will run out and the wineskins will be ruined. ³⁸No, new wine must be poured into new wineskins."

Interpreting Dreams Dictionary

Wings - *Spirit /Refreshing*
    Positive - Prophet, Spirit of God, shelter, protection, uplifting
    Negative - Demonic spirit
    Mal 4:2, Psa 91:4, Isa 40:31

    Exo 19:4 "'You yourselves have seen what I did to Egypt, and how I carried you on eagles' wings and brought you to myself.

Winter - *Barren / Withdrawn*
    Positive - Patient, abiding, retreat
    Negative - Unfruitful, cold emotions, dormant
    Zec 14:8, 1 Cor 16:6

    Prov 20:4 "The lazy man will not plow because of winter; He will beg during harvest and have nothing."

Witch - *Witchcraft / Demonic Force*
    Evil influence, seduction, non-submissive, rebellion, Jezebel spirit
    1 Sam 15:23, Rev 2:20

    Gal 3:1 "You foolish Galatians! Who has bewitched you? Before your very eyes Jesus Christ was clearly portrayed as crucified."

Wolf - *Predator / Enemy Against the Church*
    Positive - Strength, agility, leader
    Negative - False prophet, opportunist, deception, prowler, destructive force from within the Church
    Matt 7:15, John 10:10, Acts. 20:29

Jer 5:6 "Therefore a lion from the forest will attack them, a wolf from the desert will ravage them, a leopard will lie in wait near their towns to tear to pieces any who venture out, for their rebellion is great and their backslidings many."

Woman - *Holy Spirit*
    Positive - Angelic messenger
    Negative - Spirit of seduction, temptation, deception
    Pro 2:16, Matt 8:20

Acts 9:36 "At Joppa there was a certain disciple named Tabitha, which is translated Dorcas. This woman was full of good works and charitable deeds which she did. (NKJV)

Interpreting Dreams Dictionary

Wood - *Life / Protection*
Positive - Eternal, building spiritual things, growth, structure, strength
Negative - Flesh, carnal reasoning, lust, appetites of the flesh
Pro 26:20-21, Rev 9:20

1 Cor 3:12-14 "12 If any man builds on this foundation using gold, silver, costly stones, wood, hay or straw, 13 his work will be shown for what it is, because the Day will bring it to light. It will be revealed with fire, and the fire will test the quality of each man's work. 14 If what he has built survives, he will receive his reward."

Worm - *Corruption / Destruction*
Positive - Fertility, breaking down, cleansing
Negative - Lowliness, weakness, corruption, evil, disease
Psa 22:6, Mark 9:44

Isa 51:8 "For the moth will eat them up like a garment; the worm will devour them like wool. But my righteousness will last forever, my salvation through all generations."

Wrestling - *Perseverance*
Positive - Deliverance, persistence, travail
Negative - Struggle, opposition, tribulation, trial, control
Eph 6:12, 2 Tim 2:24

Gen 32:24 "So Jacob was left alone, and a man wrestled with him till daybreak."

- Y -

Yard - *See Front or Back*

Year - *Circulation / Complete Cycle*
    Positive - Specified period of blessing
    Negative - Specified period of judgement
    Job 36:11, Luke 4:19, Eze 4:5

Job 3:6 "That night—may thick darkness seize it; may it not be included among the days of the year nor be entered in any of the months."

Yoke - *Servitude / Commitment*
    Positive - Service, servant, fellowship, complete union, marriage
    Negative - Bondage to sin, enslaved, legalism
    Gen 27:40, Lev 26:13, Gal 1:5

1 Tim 6:1 "All who are under the yoke of slavery should consider their masters worthy of full respect, so that God's name and our teaching may not be slandered."

- Z -

Zion - *Dwelling Place of God / Protection*
Positive - Majesty, stability, strength, exalted, Kingdom of God, transfiguration, prophecy
Negative - Obstacle, difficulty, challenge, agony, kingdom of man
Psa 50:2, Rom 9:33

Zec 8:3 "This is what the LORD says: "I will return to Zion and dwell in Jerusalem. Then Jerusalem will be called the City of Truth, and the mountain of the LORD Almighty will be called the Holy Mountain."

Interpreting Dreams Dictionary

Colors

Black - *Lack or loss*
    Negative - Sin, darkness, ignorance, grief or in mourning, gloom, evil, famine
    Pro 7:9, Lam 5:10

    Jer 4:28 "For this shall the earth mourn, And the heavens above be black, because I have spoken. I have purposed and will not relent, Nor will I turn back from it. (NKJV)

Blue - *Revelation*
    Positive - Spiritual gift, revelation of Christ, heavenly visitation or vision
    Negative - Depression, lack of blessing, separation
    Num 4:7,9, Eze 23:6, Pro 20:30

    2 Chr 2:7 "'Send me, therefore, a man skilled to work in gold and silver, bronze and iron, and in purple, crimson and blue yarn, and experienced in the art of engraving, to work in Judah and Jerusalem with my skilled craftsmen, whom my father David provided."

Brown (Tan) - *Carnality / Flesh*
    Positive - Born again, repented, new life, renewed mind
    Negative - Lifeless, without spirit
    Nah 1:4

    1 Pet 1:24 "For, "All men are like grass, and all their glory is like the flowers of the field; the grass withers and the flowers fall,"

Gold - *Wisdom or Glory*
    Positive - Glory of God, truth, righteousness
    Negative - Self-glorification
    Jam 2:2-4, 2 Chr 16:2

    Pro 8:10 "Choose my instruction instead of silver, knowledge rather than choice gold,"

Gray - *Without Definition / Compromised*
    Positive - Wisdom, maturity, council, direction
    Negative - Unclear, vague, deception, false doctrine or teaching
    Pro 16:31

    Hos 7:9 "Foreigners sap his strength, but he does not realize it. His hair is sprinkled with gray, but he does not notice."

Green - *Life / Carnality*
    Positive - Eternal life, renewal, rejuvenation, new life, positive change, healing
    Negative - Fleshly, immature, carnal, envy, inexperience
    1 Pet 1:24, Psa 37:35

    Gen 9:3 "Everything that lives and moves will be food for you. Just as I gave you the green plants, I now give you everything."

Interpreting Dreams Dictionary

Orange - *Power / Impersonation*
    Positive - Power of God, energetic force, Holy Spirit fire, protection, purification
    Negative - Danger, caution, great jeopardy, harm, persecution
    Pro 6:27, Matt 5:22, Zec 5:2

    Acts 2:3 "They saw what seemed to be tongues of fire that separated and came to rest on each of them."

Pink - *Flesh / Mixture of Fire and Light*
    Positive - Moral, chaste, purity (white) combined with the blood of Jesus (red)
    Negative - Sensual, immoral, flesh, watered down message, lack of passion
    Rev 6:7, Exo 26:14

    Eze 36:26 "I will give you a new heart and put a new spirit in you; I will remove from you your heart of stone and give you a heart of flesh."

Purple - *God / Royalty*
    Positive - King, prince, wealth, authority, presence of God
    Negative - Political power, dishonesty, wickedness, costly
    Acts 16:14, Pro 6:27 Jud 8:26

    Luke 16:19 "There was a rich man who was dressed in purple and fine linen and lived in luxury every day."

Red - *Blood of Christ / Spirit of Conflict*
　　Positive - Passion of Christ, sacrifice, passion of heart, forgiveness, cleansing
　　Negative - Deep sins, anger, hatred, lust, conquered
　　Rev 6:4, Heb 9:11

Isa 1:18 "Come now, let us reason together," says the LORD. "Though your sins are like scarlet, they shall be as white as snow; though they are red as crimson, they shall be like wool."

Silver - *Knowledge / Purity*
　　Positive - Redemption, knowledge of God, revelation
　　Negative - Idolatry, spiritual adultery, worldly knowledge, betrayal
　　Mat 27:6, 1 Pet 1:17-18

Psa 12:6 "And the words of the LORD are flawless, like silver refined in a furnace of clay, purified seven times."

White - *Holiness / Glory*
　　Righteousness, God's majesty, cleansed, spotless, truth, innocence
　　2Kin 5:27, Isa 1:18

Rev 1:14 "His head and hair were white like wool, as white as snow, and his eyes were like blazing fire."

Yellow - *Gift / Carnality*
    Positive - Gift from or of God, light and life, family, honor
    Negative - Cowardice, false gift, timidity, fear
    Psa 68:13, 2 Tim 1:7

Pro 19:14 "Houses and wealth are inherited from parents, but a prudent wife is from the LORD."

Numbers

One - *Unity*
New, fresh start, timing, position or order, importance, deity
Gen 1:1,5; 8:13

Matt 6:33 "But seek first his kingdom and his righteousness, and all these things will be given to you as well."

Two - *Division / Unity*
Witness, judge, separate, discern, division, union, marriage, agreement, strength
Gen 1:6-8, 1 Kin 3:25, 28

Ecc 4:9-10 " ⁹ Two are better than one, because they have a good return for their work: ¹⁰ If one falls down, his friend can help him up. But pity the man who falls and has no one to help him up!"

Three - *Strength*
Obey, conformity, imitate, likeness, tradition, divine fullness, Godhead
Gen 1:9, 11, 13, Eph 3:19

Rom 8:29 "For those God foreknew he also predestined to be conformed to the likeness of his Son, that he might be the firstborn among many brothers."

Four - *Reign*
World, earth, creation, creative work, territory
Gen 1:16, 18-19, Rev 5:9, Isa 58:6-10

Luke 13:29 "People will come from east and west and north and south, and will take their places at the feast in the kingdom of God."

Five - *Service / Ministries / Completeness*
Works, service, atonement, grace, fullness, five-fold ministry, bondage
Gen 1:20, 23, Lev 27:31, Matt 25:2

1 Sam 17:40 "Then he took his staff in his hand, chose five smooth stones from the stream, put them in the pouch of his shepherd's bag and, with his sling in his hand, approached the Philistine."

Six - *Man*
Flesh, carnal, idolatry, Satan, image of self, work, toil and strain, curse, beast
Gen 1:26, 31, Num 35:15, Pet 3:8

Rev 13:18 "This calls for wisdom. If anyone has insight, let him calculate the number of the beast, for it is man's number. His number is 666."

Seven - *Completion / God*
  Finished work, mature, perfection, rest
  Gen 2:1-3, Matt 18:21-22

  Rev 1:20 "The mystery of the seven stars that you saw in my right hand and of the seven golden lampstands is this: The seven stars are the angels of the seven churches, and the seven lampstands are the seven churches."

Eight - *New Beginning*
  Sanctify, manifest, reveal, death, resurrection life, liberty
  Gen 17:12, 1 Pet 3:20-21, 2 Chr 29:17

  2 Pet 2:5 "and did not spare the ancient world, but saved Noah, one of eight people, a preacher of righteousness, bringing in the flood on the world of the ungodly;" (NKJV)

Nine - *Harvest / Reaping*
  Fruit of the Spirit, gifts of the Spirit, fruitfulness, fullness of development, finality, maturity
  Luke 17:17, Gal 5:22-23

  1 Cor 12:7-11 "[7]Now to each one the manifestation of the Spirit is given for the common good. [8]To one there is given through the Spirit the message of wisdom, to another the message of knowledge by means of the same Spirit, [9]to another faith by the same Spirit, to another gifts of healing by that one Spirit, [10]to another miraculous powers, to another prophecy, to another distinguishing between spirits, to another speaking in different kinds of tongues, and to still another the interpretation of tongues. [11]All these are the work of one and the same Spirit, and he gives them to each one, just as he determines."

Ten - *Government / Completion*
   Trial, measure, testing, tithe, order, law
   Lev 27:32, Rev 2:10

   Exo 34:28 "Moses was there with the LORD forty days and forty nights without eating bread or drinking water. And he wrote on the tablets the words of the covenant—the Ten Commandments."

Note on numbers 11 - 19: It is important to note that the numbers 11 - 19 represent the opposites of the numbers 1 - 9. For example, 2 means to *divide*, 12 means to *join*

Eleven - *Division / Ending*
   Finish, final, last, stop
   Gen 27:9, Deu 11:8

   Matt 28:16 "Then the eleven disciples went to Galilee, to the mountain where Jesus had told them to go."

Twelve - *Joined / Fullness*
   Divine government, apostolic fullness, discipleship, oversight, unity
   Rev 22:2, Exo 15:27

   Luke 9:1-2 "¹When Jesus had called the Twelve together, he gave them power and authority to drive out all demons and to cure diseases, ²and he sent them out to preach the kingdom of God and to heal the sick."

Interpreting Dreams Dictionary

Thirteen - *Weakness*
   Revolution, rebellion, rejection, backsliding
   Gen 14:4, Est 9:11

   1 Kin 7:1 "It took Solomon thirteen years, however, to complete the construction of his palace."

Fourteen - *Recreate / Retirement*
   Disciple, servant, reproduce, passover
   Exo 12:6, 1 Kin 8:65

   Num 9:5 "and they did so in the Desert of Sinai at twilight on the fourteenth day of the first month. The Israelites did everything just as the LORD commanded Moses."

Fifteen - *Deliverance / Freedom*
   Grace, liberty, honor
   Lev 23:6-7, Hos 3:2, Gen 7:20

   Isa 38:5 ""Go and tell Hezekiah, 'This is what the LORD, the God of your father David, says: I have heard your prayer and seen your tears; I will add fifteen years to your life."

Sixteen - *Free-Spirited*
   Free from the law, without boundaries, salvation
   Acts 27:34, 37-38

   Rom 8:2 "because through Christ Jesus the law of the Spirit of life set me free from the law of sin and death."

Seventeen - *Incomplete / Immature*
  Undeveloped or underdeveloped, premature, unfinished, childish, naive
  Gen 37:2

  Jer 32:9 "so I bought the field at Anathoth from my cousin Hanamel and weighed out for him seventeen shekels of silver."

Eighteen - *Bondage to Past*
  Judgement, destruction, captivity, overcome or overwhelmed
  Luke 13:4; 13:11-16

  Jud 10:7-8 "he became angry with them. He sold them into the hands of the Philistines and the Ammonites, ⁸ who that year shattered and crushed them. For eighteen years they oppressed all the Israelites on the east side of the Jordan in Gilead, the land of the Amorites."

Nineteen - *Barren*
  Ashamed, barren in the flesh or spirit, repentant, absence of self-righteousness
  Rom 6:21

  2 Sam 2:30 "Then Joab returned from pursuing Abner and assembled all his men. Besides Asahel, nineteen of David's men were found missing."

Twenty - *Approved / Accepted*
Tried or proven, redemption, rescue, protection
Exo 30:12-14, Gen 18:31, Psa 68:17-18

Gen 31:38-42 "I have been with you for twenty years now. Your sheep and goats have not miscarried, nor have I eaten rams from your flocks. I did not bring you animals torn by wild beasts; I bore the loss myself. And you demanded payment from me for whatever was stolen by day or night. This was my situation: The heat consumed me in the daytime and the cold at night, and sleep fled from my eyes. It was like this for the twenty years I was in your household. I worked for you fourteen years for your two daughters and six years for your flocks, and you changed my wages ten times. If the God of my father, the God of Abraham and the Fear of Isaac, had not been with me, you would surely have sent me away empty-handed. But God has seen my hardship and the toil of my hands, and last night he rebuked you."

Interpreting Dreams Dictionary

Twenty-four - *Consecration*
Maturity, priesthood, perfection in government
1 Chr 24:3-5

Rev 4:4-5, 9-11 "⁴Surrounding the throne were twenty-four other thrones, and seated on them were twenty-four elders. They were dressed in white and had crowns of gold on their heads. ⁵From the throne came flashes of lightning, rumblings and peals of thunder. Before the throne, seven lamps were blazing. These are the seven spirits of God.
⁹Whenever the living creatures give glory, honor and thanks to him who sits on the throne and who lives for ever and ever, ¹⁰the twenty-four elders fall down before him who sits on the throne, and worship him who lives for ever and ever. They lay their crowns before the throne and say: ¹¹"You are worthy, our Lord and God, to receive glory and honor and power, for you created all things, and by your will they were created and have their being."

Thirty - *Beginning of Maturity*
Ministry accepted, maturity, blood of Christ
Gen 41:16, Num 4:3

Luke 3:23 "Now Jesus himself was about thirty years old when he began his ministry. He was the son, so it was thought, of Joseph,"

Forty - *Testing*
Trial, cleansing, wilderness, supply, faith
Gen 7:4, Exo 16:35

Matt 4:1-2 " ¹Then Jesus was led by the Spirit into the desert to be tempted by the devil. ²After fasting forty days and forty nights, he was hungry."

Fifty - *Pentecost*
Jubilee, liberty, freedom, Holy Spirit
1 Kin 18:4, Luke 9:14

> *Lev 23:16 "Count off fifty days up to the day after the seventh Sabbath, and then present an offering of new grain to the LORD."*

Seventy - *Multitude*
Increase, restoration, transference, multiplication
Num 11:16-25, Eze 8:11

> *Luke 10:1 "After these things the Lord appointed seventy others also, and sent them two by two before His face into every city and place where He Himself was about to go." (NKJV)*

Hundred - *Fullness*
Full measure, full restoration, full reward
Gen 26:12

> *Mark 10:29-30 " [29]"I tell you the truth," Jesus replied, "no one who has left home or brothers or sisters or mother or father or children or fields for me and the gospel [30]will fail to receive a hundred times as much in this present age (homes, brothers, sisters, mothers, children and fields - and with them, persecutions) and in the age to come, eternal life."*

Thousand - *Maturity*
Being fully prepared, maturity in service and judgment
Jos 3:3-4, Eph 4:13, 1 Sam 17:5

Rev 20:6 "Blessed and holy are those who have part in the first resurrection. The second death has no power over them, but they will be priests of God and of Christ and will reign with him for a thousand years."